THE
FIREPROOF
RETIREMENT
PLAN

THE FIREPROOF RETIREMENT PLAN
A Safe Way to Protect Your Assets, Preserve Your Future, and Provide for
Your Family

ISBN (paperback): 978-1-964046-34-1
ISBN (ebook): 978-1-964046-57-0

Expert Press
www.ExpertPress.net

Editing by Elaina Robbins
Copyediting by Wendy Lukasiewicz
Proofreading by Abby Kendall
Text design and composition by Emily Fritz
Cover design by Casey Fritz

THE
FIREPROOF
RETIREMENT
PLAN

A SAFE WAY TO PROTECT YOUR ASSETS, PRESERVE YOUR FUTURE, AND PROVIDE FOR YOUR FAMILY

AL MARTINEZ

DEDICATION

I want to thank my mom, Annie Martinez, for trusting me to help her with her retirement plan thirty years ago. Born December 20, 1997, she is ninety-six years old as this book is being written.

CONTENTS

ACKNOWLEDGMENTS

Thank you to Dave Steinke, my former coworker with the US Forest Service, for helping me fine-tune the fire-fighting sections of this book.

STANDARD FIRE ORDERS

F Fight fire aggressively but provide for safety first.
RETIREMENT EQUIVALENT: Pay yourself first to someday have a good retirement nest egg.

I Initiate all actions based on current and expected fire behavior.
RETIREMENT EQUIVALENT: Invest regularly to eliminate the uncertainty of your market's unexpected behavior.

R Recognize current weather conditions and obtain forecast.
RETIREMENT EQUIVALENT: Keep a budget and track your expenses.

E   Ensure instructions are given and understood.
RETIREMENT EQUIVALENT: Create and follow a
plan to spend less than what you earn.

O   Obtain current information on fire status.
RETIREMENT EQUIVALENT: To prepare for
retirement, pay off debts and save at least 20
percent of your earnings.

R   Remain in communication with crew members,
your supervisor, and adjoining forces.
RETIREMENT EQUIVALENT: Work with a
financial professional to keep you up-to-date on
money matters.

D   Determine safety zones and escape routes.
RETIREMENT EQUIVALENT: Protect yourself and
your family with insurance products.

E   Establish lookouts in potentially hazardous
situations.
RETIREMENT EQUIVALENT: Create an
emergency fund for potential unplanned market
events.

R Retain control at all times.
RETIREMENT EQUIVALENT: Work with a financial professional to maintain control of your assets.

S Stay alert, keep calm, think clearly, act decisively.
RETIREMENT EQUIVALENT: Keep a level head about purchases. Invest in assets that will appreciate and not depreciate.

INTRODUCTION

"Al, take the limbs off the lower end of this tree," my crew boss said, pointing at an Engleman spruce near a pile of brush. "Trim it up so the fire on the ground here won't climb it." Lit by the harsh headlamps of the crew and the orange glow of the nearby forest fire, Dave looked larger than life. Many years of tough experiences as a firefighter were etched onto his stern face.

"On it!" I called, trying to look confident as I stomped on a stray glowing coal within the fire line. My crew and I had dug a handline[1] around a quarter-acre fire in the San Juan Mountains of southern Colorado. It was my first real fire, and my stomach had been in knots since about an hour before, when the sun set. My small crew had headed to the blaze, stumbling around as we hiked cross country in the dark, sniffing for smoke to

---

1   A hand-dug fire line of clear dirt meant to stop a fire.

guide us. We had been crossing logs and rock outcroppings, unsure of where we were going, and I had already nearly twisted my ankle on a tree root.

As Dave doled out other tasks to the rest of the crew, I turned toward my assignment. The pretty Engleman spruce tree stood twenty-five to thirty feet tall within the fire line. A ways behind it, I could narrowly make out the bare, blackened patch where lightning had struck and started the fire.

"Okay," I whispered, getting out my Pulaski[2] and taking a deep breath. "I've got this." I started limbing up the tree with the axe end of my Pulaski while trying to keep my hands from shaking. Maybe Dave would walk over and say, "Wow! Great job, Al," and I smiled a little as I created a pile of discarded branches.

Unfortunately, I was making a pile of discarded branches on the wrong side of the fire line. I hadn't seen the embers that were creeping under the forest litter near my pile of branches. By the time I noticed the orange glow on the ground, it was too late. I stepped back and gasped in horror as the fire ran right up the tree, then . . .

Whoosh!

The entire Engleman spruce exploded, shooting embers and flames thirty to forty feet into the air. The crew stopped working and hooted and hollered at what I

---

2   A Pulaski is a tool that firefighters use. It has an axe on one side and a heavy-duty chisel hoe on the other that can be used to tear things apart.

had done. My face burned with shame. Someone clapped me on the shoulder. I turned around to see Dave grinning at me. "I'm fired, aren't I?"

Dave laughed. "It's not a big deal. We've all done it. Next time, though, throw those branches *outside* the fire line rather than straight into the embers."

Luckily, the fire didn't go anywhere. But even though Dave was nice about it, that mistake under other circumstances could have been catastrophic. Decades later, when I retired from firefighting and got into finance, I remembered that story because it seems so similar to what happens to many soon-to-be retirees.

Most people think if you put your money in the market and grow it when you're young, everything will turn out okay. You do what you're told, cutting the branches off that tree and tossing them aside, feeling good about yourself. And yes, at the beginning, that's what you need to do. You need to save your money, diversify, and take risks.

But as you approach your fifties, things start to change. There are more career years behind you than there are in front of you. You've been keeping your head down, working hard, and cutting off all those limbs. But where have you been putting them? Have you been stacking them too close to the embers and taking on too much risk? Your financial stability could explode right in front of you precisely when you're set to retire.

Let's say you work hard for decades, doing what you think is right. Then you come up for air two years before retirement. Your brush pile is sitting next to a fiery market, the market takes a huge downturn, and now you're 20 to 30 percent in the hole. You've lost that money, and you don't have enough time to get it back. I've been working as a Certified Financial Fiduciary and Ed Slott Elite IRA specialist for several years, and I see this all the time.

Night shift

If you're like most of my clients, you don't know how to manage your finances in a way that's going to prevent your own personal forest fire. That's why I wrote this book. If you're still at the beginning of your career, this book isn't for you. This book is for people who are a few years out of retirement and need a new mindset. Those are the folks I work with most often, teaching them that as you near retirement, it's more important to convert your mindset from *risk* to *safety*. You must preserve your money rather than risk it in the name of growth.

This book examines how to make your money last despite a volatile market, how to factor in inflation and taxation, and how to plan an appropriate withdrawal rate. It will also cover long-term care and mortality—two areas that aren't fun to think about but are still necessary.

Yes, I wholeheartedly agree that investing money in the beginning of your working career is a sensible thing to do. But so many experts tell you to keep investing when that can be like stacking limbs next to the embers. The world is full of financial infernos, and as you near retirement, you need to plan your strategy to put them out. I hope *The Fireproof Retirement Plan* helps you shift your mindset from a riskier investment approach to one that will help you enjoy a secure, fun retirement—free of fires.

Yellowstone fire

CHAPTER 1

THE FIREPROOF LONGEVITY CHALLENGE – THE RISKS OF LIVING LONGER

In early July 1988, my twenty-person crew was assigned to a massive fire in Yellowstone National Park. We were transported via the Bell 206 helicopter, which is configured to hold five passengers and one pilot. Our destination was a section of the fire near a bunch of lakes. I still remember taking in that devastating aerial view. Vast swaths of fire raged below in a shimmering patchwork of orange, blue, and green. We couldn't hear each other talk over the thumping helicopter rotors, so my crewmates and I glanced at each other, grimacing. We knew we would be here for a good long while. This fire was enormous.

The days seemed to blend together as my crew and I battled hard. We had some close calls with falling trees that collapsed from burned-out roots and nearly crushed us under burning wood and ash. Other crews actually experienced fatalities in this way, their bodies flown via helicopter for burials back home. Each time, we grieved and worried we may be next.

Come September, we were still in the park when a falling tree nearly crushed my crewmate Dan. We were working a section of fire when we heard a dreadful groan. I leapt back, then watched as Dan dove out of the way of a toppling tree in the nick of time.

"Are you all right?" I asked, helping him up. We were both shaking.

"The longer we're here," he panted, "the more chances we have to get killed. Every day this darn fire goes on is a day we could end up smashed like a bug."

Eventually, it started to snow, and my family had to send me boots and a winter jacket. Snowfall on a fire may temporarily suppress it for a day or two, but it doesn't extinguish it entirely. That fire persisted even after it had snowed. We finally did get it under control, though, and hundreds of thousands of acres of Yellowstone forest were burned up in the end.

Most fires last maybe five to fourteen days, somewhere in there. This fire went on for just under four months.[3] When we finally flew out of there, I clapped Dan on the shoulder, and we grinned at each other in relief. We had made it, but Dan was right—every day we spent up there was a risk.

When you're on a fire for a long period of time, your risk factor goes up. The longer you're out there, the more you're exposed to different hazards, whether it be falling trees or tripping over something in the dark. In retirement, the more years that pass, the more chances you have of encountering a problem. Longer lifespans are a wonderful thing, but the longer you live, the longer you need to support yourself.

In this chapter, we'll go over some of the different complications that can arise as life expectancy increases. I'll cover some of the biggest mistakes people make when trying to fireproof their finances, and I'll share two essential strategies for elongating the lifespan of your finances. By the end of this chapter, you should have a much better idea of how to protect your retirement savings from financial fires year after year, as long as you live.

Longer Life, More Risks

According to the US Census Bureau, as of July 1, 2021, there are about seventy-six million baby boomers, about

---

3   "1988 Fires," Yellowstone National Park (National Park Service), Accessed March 27, 2024, https://www.nps.gov/yell/learn/nature/1988-fires.htm.

23 percent of the US population,[4] who are either in retirement or approaching retirement. At the time of writing, a large chunk of that baby boomer group is expected to turn sixty-five.[5] The enduring longevity of this group carries immense significance.

That's a profound demographic shift as this sizable portion of our population ages. In 2015, a sixty-five-year-old male had a life expectancy of around eighty-three years.[6] In 2024, a sixty-five-year-old male has a life expectancy somewhere around eighty-eight.[7] Sixty-year-old women were expected to live to eighty-four in 2004,[8] and in 2024, they're expected to live to approximately eighty-six.[9] It's a trend my mother, born in 1927, exemplified.

4 "Annual Estimates of the Resident Population for Selected Age Groups by Sex for the United States: April 1, 2020 to July 1, 2022," US Census Bureau, Accessed March 28, 2024, https://www2.census.gov/programs-surveys/popest/tables/2020-2022/national/asrh/nc-est2022-agesex.xlsx.

5 Lorie Konish, "As Baby Boomers Hit 'Peak 65' This Year, What the Retirement Age Should Be Is Up for Debate," CNBC, February 8, 2024, Accessed March 28, 2024, https://www.cnbc.com/2024/02/08/baby-boomers-hit-peak-65-in-2024-why-retirement-age-is-in-question.html.

6 "Life Expectancy and Healthy Life Expectancy at Age 65," Health at a Glance 2017: OECD Indicators, OECD Publishing, https://doi.org/10.1787/health_glance-2017-74-en.

7 "Life Expectancy at 65," OECD, Accessed March 29, 2024, https://data.oecd.org/healthstat/life-expectancy-at-65.htm.

8 Elizabeth Arias, PhD, "United States Life Tables, 2004" National Vital Statistics Reports, Volume 56, Number 9, December 28, 2007, https://www.cdc.gov/nchs/data/nvsr/nvsr56/nvsr56_09.pdf.

9 "Retirement & Survivors Benefits: Life Expectancy Calculator," Social Security Administration, Accessed March 3, 2024, https://www.ssa.gov/cgi-bin/longevity.cgi.

The longer you live, the longer you're likely to live. This means that at sixty-five, you could be looking at reaching eighty-six or eighty-seven. If you make it to eighty, you may end up enjoying life well into your nineties. With each passing year, life expectancy seems to stretch a bit further. It's a reflection of our times. Thanks to better nutrition and health care, people are enjoying longer lives than ever before.

But all that time is time that you have to pay for.

The Challenges of Extended Retirement

Just like firefighters working a long-term fire, the longer you're around in retirement, the more chances problems can occur. You've got to make that nest egg last, and that's difficult. I've had clients who had a nest egg, but they were so concerned about spending it too quickly that their retirements were far from fun. They would avoid turning on lights or force themselves to eat simple meals like canned sardines—not because they couldn't afford better, but because they were afraid of living too long and running out of money. Nobody dreams of a retirement like that.

Such retirees want to save their money, not only to account for longevity but to plan for potential costs associated with longevity. And there are a lot of risks to worry about. There's market risk, deflation risk, withdrawal rate risks, sequence of returns risk, long-term care risks, mortality risks, inflation risks, taxation risks, and regulatory risks. We'll unpack some of these as the book continues, but the point is that you become more likely to encounter these risks the longer you're around.

Mortality risk in particular is one I know all too well. Over thirty years ago, my father developed cancer and died at age sixty-two. He was about to retire, and he had always handled the finances. My mother, who was around the same age and was always the homemaker, was left stranded. Her income took a major hit once my father's paycheck stopped coming in. You can hear the full story in my YouTube video at 1:35.[10]

This is a scenario I see all too often with my clients. One spouse passes away either right before or during retirement, leaving the surviving partner financially vulnerable. One spouse may have had a pension from a large company (an arrangement that's becoming increasingly rare), but sometimes this pension was designed solely for the benefit of the deceased spouse without provisions for its continuation to the surviving partner. As a result, the surviving spouse finds themselves in a precarious position.

Luckily, in my mom's case, I was able to help with her financial planning. At the time of writing, she's ninety-six and thriving, still living comfortably thanks to her smart choices and financial setup. Plus, she's been

10   https://www.youtube.com/watch?v=4f6t0PTk5Ug

debt free all these years. I'll tell you how I did it in a minute.

Withdrawal Rates

Normally, a fire that lasts a long time is far riskier than a quick blaze. The longer it stretches, the more issues can arise. So you want to stick to a financial plan that takes that into account, which has traditionally meant adhering to a specific withdrawal rate.

In the traditional financial services sector, particularly within brokerage firms, there has long been a rule of thumb spanning the past three to four decades: If your portfolio contains your life savings or retirement funds, you should withdraw around 4 percent upon retirement. The "4 percent rule" suggests that withdrawing 4 percent of your funds throughout retirement should sustain your finances for your entire life. But despite our best efforts to secure our financial future and retreat to where we think we're safe, unforeseen economic events can still pose substantial risks. That's why, in this section, I'll cover the sequence of returns risk, the 4 percent rule, and the withdrawal strategy that will actually work over a long period of time.

Before we move on, let's talk about the example retirement savings amounts I use in this book. I like to choose round numbers so people can understand the concepts of these different strategies, but keep in mind that these numbers don't necessarily reflect what the average person needs to retire. I might choose an example of $500,000 because it's easy to work with. If you have $500,000 and you make 5 percent in interest, both of us can mentally calculate that to be $25,000. If I were to choose $142,000 as an example, calculating 5 percent of that can make some people's heads spin.

Sequence of Returns Risk

To understand withdrawal rates, you first have to understand the sequence of returns. The sequence of returns is a mathematically proven concept commonly discussed in retirement finances. It boils down to this: If you have a retirement account with a planned withdrawal rate, and the market experiences downturns during the initial years of withdrawals, the longevity of your funds can be significantly impacted. In other words, the market during your first few years of retirement matters a whole lot.

When I first talk to potential clients, many tell me they're confident they can sustain a 6 percent withdrawal rate based on their historical average returns. I'll counter with a hypothetical example of, say, someone who has a million-dollar account and starts withdrawing 6 percent annually. I pull out my handy sequence of returns risk chart and show them what this would look like.

SEQUENCE OF RETURNS RISK

Distribution Phase: $1,000,000 Beginning Balance

Age	INVESTOR A Annual Return[1]	Portfolio Year-End Value[3]	Withdrawals	INVESTOR B Annual Return[2]	Portfolio Year-End Value[3]
65	-9.03%	$844,700.00	($65,000.00)	13.48%	$1,069,800.00
66	-11.85%	$679,603.05	($65,000.00)	31.15%	$1,338,042.70
67	-21.97%	$465,294.26	($65,000.00)	15.89%	$1,485,657.69
68	28.36%	$532,251.71	($65,000.00)	2.10%	$1,451,856.50
69	10.74%	$524,415.55	($65,000.00)	14.82%	$1,602,021.63
70	4.83%	$484,744.82	($65,000.00)	25.94%	$1,952,586.04
71	15.61%	$495,413.48	($65,000.00)	-36.55%	$1,173,915.84
72	5.48%	$457,562.14	($65,000.00)	5.48%	$1,173,246.43
73	-36.55%	$225,323.18	($65,000.00)	15.61%	$1,291,390.20
74	25.94%	$218,772.01	($65,000.00)	4.83%	$1,288,764.34
75	14.82%	$186,194.02	($65,000.00)	10.74%	$1,362,177.64
76	2.10%	$125,104.10	($65,000.00)	28.36%	$1,683,491.21
77	15.89%	$79,983.14	($65,000.00)	-21.97%	$1,248,628.19
78	31.15%	$39,897.89	($65,000.00)	-11.85%	$1,035,665.75
79	13.48%	-$19,723.88	($65,000.00)	-9.03%	$877,145.13

5.93%	Arithmetic Average[4]	5.93%
4.14%	Geometric Average[5]	4.14%

If you have the majority of your nest egg in the market, the date you choose as your Retirement Date could have a devastating impact on your "golden years" depending on the date you select. Research has shown that **it is imperative to the longevity of your retirement plan not to incur losses during the initial phase of retirement**, also known as the "Critical Phase." The report above illustrates the alarming effects and the importance of "Sequence Of Returns," the order in which losses/gains are sustained in an investment portfolio.

[1] S&P 500 dividend reinvested returns from 2000 to 2014 (DOES NOT include deductions for investment fees) obtained from the Federal Reserve database in St. Louis (FRED) and reported by New York University - Source: http://pages.stern.nyu.edu/~adamodar/New_Home_Page/datafile/histretSP.html
[2] S&P 500 dividend reinvested returns from 2014 to 2000 (in reverse of 1)
[3] Year-end account value after gains/losses and withdrawals
[4] Arithmetic Average: The sum of a series of numbers divided by the count of that series of numbers. (Investopedia) This method is used frequently by portfolio managers to advertise fund performance because it produces a higher reported return than Geometric Average, but it is the incorrect method for evaluating investment returns because it does not account for actual changes in account values.
[5] Geometric Average: The average of a set of products, the calculation of which is commonly used to determine the performance results of an investment or portfolio. The geometric mean must be used when working with percentages (which are derived from values), whereas the standard arithmetic mean will work with the values themselves (Investopedia). This is the correct method to use when calculating investment performance.

Disclosure: This illustration does not represent investing, tax, or legal advice.

This chart shows two scenarios: a market downturn akin to 2008 early in retirement, and a market performing exceptionally well during the initial years of retirement. If you have $100,000 saved up, but you lose 40 percent of it to market volatility, you're left with $60,000. If you continue withdrawing funds at the same rate, you have an estimated 85 percent chance of depleting your funds before the end of your life. On the other hand, if the market performs well during the early years of withdrawals, you stand a better chance of maintaining your funds over your lifetime, assuming a reasonable withdrawal rate (4 percent or lower).

In essence, the sequence of returns plays a pivotal role in determining whether your retirement savings will last or not. When I explain this to clients, they quickly see how their chosen withdrawal rate can influence the sustainability of their retirement savings more than they thought.

Debunking the 4 Percent Rule

Because of the sequence of returns, the 4 percent withdrawal rate, which used to be the rule of thumb, is no longer a rule of thumb. This rule held true before the early 2000s when the internet wasn't as advanced as it is today. At that time, you could sustainably withdraw around 4 percent. With the advent of the internet, however, the markets have become so volatile and influenced by so many external factors. Renowned economists such as Dr. Wade Pfau, Tom Hegna, and Roger Ibbotson have demonstrated that the traditional 4 percent sustainability concept is not applicable today; the percentage is considerably lower now.

Let's say you were sixty-four years old in 2001, ready to retire with a substantial nest egg. You began drawing your money as the markets plummeted, and your savings depleted alarmingly fast. Withdrawing money wasn't sustainable thanks to the market and sequence of returns.

Finding a Sustainable Withdrawal Strategy

The notion of a sustainable 4 percent withdrawal rate is no longer valid, and the sequence of returns can throw a wrench into seemingly solid plans. You might be wondering, "What's the appropriate withdrawal rate, then?" Let's consult with the experts.

Economist Dr. Wade Pfau believes that the sustainable withdrawal rate has significantly decreased compared to previous years because those years didn't encounter both low interest rates and high stock market valuations at the same time.[11] Tom Hegna says that the bulletproof rate is only 2 percent.[12] Roger Ibbotson,

---

11   Jane Wollman Rusoff, "Wade Pfau: Pandemic Tears Up 4% Rule," *ThinkAdvisor*, February 10, 2021, https://www.thinkadvisor.com/2020/04/14/wade-pfau-virus-crisis-has-slashed-4-rule-nearly-in-half/.

12   "Tom Hegna," Facebook, Accessed January 28, 2020, https://web.facebook.com/TomHegnaSpeaks/posts/2779911268783210/.

a financial professor at Yale School of Management, suggests that relying on withdrawing 4 percent of your retirement savings annually, especially in the early stages of retirement, could expose your funds to risk during a bear market.[13] Across experts, the current rule of thumb suggests a withdrawal rate closer to 2.8 percent. This is for a retiree aiming for a 90 percent chance of hitting their retirement income goal over thirty years with a 40 percent equity portfolio. It's important to note that at that 2.8 percent lower withdrawal rate, a retiree would need to boost savings by 42.9 percent to keep withdrawing the same amount annually from their portfolio as they would with a 4 percent rate on a smaller portfolio.[14]

At that point, the critical question is whether you can realistically live on a 2.8 percent withdrawal. The answer? Not usually. Even if you have $1 million saved up, a 2.8 percent withdrawal equates to $28,000 annually. Unless your dream retirement consists of eating canned tuna, that's not going to be enough, especially for two people or those living in more expensive locales. So while a 2.8 percent withdrawal rate may theoretically preserve your savings, it falls short of sustaining your lifestyle.

---

13   Impact Partners Contributor, "How Does Sequence of Returns Risk Impact Your Retirement?" *Forbes*, July 22, 2019, https://www.forbes.com/sites/impactpartners/2019/07/22/how-does-sequence-of-returns-risk-impact-your-retirement/?sh=7d23d54b50ee.

14   David Blanchett, Michael Finke, and Wade D. Pfau, "Low Bond Yields and Safe Portfolio Withdrawal Rates," Morningstar Investment Management, January 21, 2013, https://s3.amazonaws.com/static.contentres.com/media/documents/6bc2b7ed-8f1c-4f33-8f81-d8db3fb444fe.pdf.

This may all sound bleak, but don't worry—your options aren't reduced to running out of money or living like a pauper. In chapter 3, I'll share my strategies for making your money last.

Fireproofing Your Funds

The longer a fire burns, the crazier things can get. The longer you live, the more risk your retirement funds must bear. That 1988 fire in Yellowstone burned for months and months, causing irreparable damage and claiming lives. Had it been a shorter fire, no matter how violent, it probably wouldn't have resulted in that kind of devastation.

As you plan your retirement, you could make a misstep and lose a tidy portion of your saved money. And once you retire, you have to rely on that money because your working life is over. That money provides your income, and if you lose a bunch of it, your income will be reduced. Learning about an appropriate withdrawal rate is a huge part of planning for retirement.

The next chapter will discuss risk factors that can make your retirement plans go up in smoke.

Fire moving down a hillside.

CHAPTER 2

BURNOVER—THE MARKET AND INFLATION

Fire operates on three fundamental elements: oxygen, heat, and fuel. This is the fire triangle. When these elements align, a fire can sustain itself. Early on in my firefighting career, I didn't understand how fires work and how fires can change, but boy, did I learn fast.

I'll never forget the Taylor Park Fire in the Gunnison National Forest in Colorado that I worked early in my career. When we got to the site, we learned that this fire was 150 to 200 acres—sizable enough to require multiple fire crews.

"We're going to dig a fire line to cut the fire off this way," the crew boss shouted. Bill was another hardened firefighting veteran. "But we gotta hurry. The winds might change on us, so if worse comes to worst, we can use a meadow back down the fire line as a safety zone."

The meadow had no flammable material and would protect us from the fire if we ran into trouble. We got straight to work, and as the day progressed into the hot mid-afternoon, I heard Bill's radio crackle to life. "The fire has altered its course," the Overhead Team declared through static. "It's heading directly toward you. Flames reaching one hundred and fifty to two hundred feet. We've got a burnover situation. You've got to get out of there."

My heart dropped. *Burnover* meant the fire would engulf everything around it—including us. There was no time to lose.

We sprinted down the fire line to our safety zone in the meadow. This was no fun jog. The fire was racing toward us, and you could tell. The air was suffocatingly hot and smoky, and the wind was howling all around us. For three to four hours, we felt like we were inside a volcano as we dodged embers the size of pine cones and struggled to breathe through our bandanas. We didn't need to use our fire shelters since the meadow was large enough to keep us from the searing heat, but that didn't stop our fear from looming as thick as the scorching heat and pitch-black smoke.

In these situations, you learn if you want to continue to fight fires for a living. You're either so overwhelmed with fear that you want nothing to do with this danger, or you're so pumped up on adrenaline that you want to get in there and battle. Those who feel the need to escape usually don't last in firefighting; they simply go on to some other career. As for me, I liked the rush.

I had a lot of time to think during that Colorado inferno.

Most of the time, fires are predictable. By now I had a few months under my belt, and I thought I knew how they worked. But that day, I learned something new. Every once in a while, factors like sudden wind events can alter fire behavior, making them fickle and dangerous. I was experiencing a stark wake-up call of how quickly a fire can escalate and threaten one's life.

Within a mere four-hour period, that fire swelled from roughly 150 acres to a staggering 10,000 acres. Our crew, safe in our designated safety zone, got out alive.

Markets and inflation rates are much the same as forest fires. Everything is fine until the wind shifts and the flames become uncontrollable. That's when you need your safety zone. So in this chapter, our focus shifts toward how you, as a soon-to-be or already retiree, should approach the market and inflation. We'll cover the financial aspect of managing market volatility, safety strategies, and implementing firebreak strategies. You'll also learn about inflation and how it can affect the buying power of your retirement savings over time.

Fire bumping into a dozer line.

Market Inferno Unleashed: Market Volatility in Your Golden Years

In uncertain markets, retirees tend to get nervous. For one, they don't feel like they've saved enough money because it's going out faster than what they planned. If you couple that with market risk, which decreases the value of accounts by sheer market losses alone, people are feeling more squeezed than ever. I've seen this in cycles. In 2001, people at age sixty-two, sixty-three, or sixty-five were getting ready to retire, when all of a sudden their portfolio was cut in half, and they were left scrambling. It happened again in 2008 and 2020. But in between crisis times, people lose track of risks and get complacent.

Back in 2008, I had a client who was a lifelong bachelor with $500,000 saved up in a 401(k). Mr. Jones was sixty-three years old and getting ready to retire from his job with the city. "My knees have started to bother me," he told me ruefully. "It's time I sat down." He had a pension and his 401(k) that would comfortably fund his retirement.

Then the market crashed. Almost overnight, Mr. Jones's 401(k) lost 40 percent. His retirement amount had suddenly gone down to $320,000.

My client was faced with two choices. He hadn't been planning on drawing from a $320,000 account to support himself, especially with potential knee surgery on the horizon. He could either live on a reduced lifestyle or work another few years until his account recovered. Mr. Jones decided to keep working, and in six years he ended up retiring at age sixty-nine with the income he needed to live comfortably.

During that tough time, Mr. Jones and many of my other clients had to change their retirement plan because the market losses dictated that they had to make some drastic choices. And that wasn't a one-time thing. Our markets will continue to fluctuate, and the timing of these fluctuations can leave people who want to retire without the means to do so—unless they plan accordingly.

I also had clients who had put their money in a different type of account—one that shielded the funds from the crash—and didn't have to make these tough decisions. The trick is to choose retirement investments that aren't subject to the market at all. These accounts are, as a firefighter would say, the designated safe zones. We'll discuss them in the next chapter.

During a downturn, there are typically two approaches to investment. One perspective, often advocated by brokerage firms, is to stay invested in the market and weather the storm. Alternatively, another viewpoint suggests minimizing losses by implementing stop-loss measures, such as converting assets into cash to prevent big losses.

This latter strategy might not be sensible for younger individuals with more time to recover from market downturns. But for people who will soon depend on their investment portfolios to sustain their livelihood, preserving capital becomes the most important thing. Transitioning the bulk of your assets into safer options can mitigate market risks and safeguard financial security during retirement. A financial advisor will help you protect your assets this way *before* rather than *during* the inferno.

Can I Play the Market Later in Life?

Not all market fluctuations are bad. There can also be good market fluctuations. Amid market volatility, investors often recognize opportunities for potential gains. Even during uncertain times, people can choose particular avenues that will capitalize on market upswings and mitigate downside risks. Specialized financial products offer a means to participate in market growth without exposing oneself to market downturns.

People who are in the retirement stage of their lives can still benefit from positive market fluctuations. Obviously, you shouldn't gamble money you can't afford to lose, but assuming you've set up a secure means of retirement income, you can take some moderate risk with what's left over. This is important. Only retirees or soon-to-be retirees who have the basics covered and can afford to lose some money should play the market. With those extra funds, retirees can assume some risk or try to grow their money, knowing that if they do make a mistake, it won't affect their lifestyle.

Even during a downturn, if you're nearing retirement and have safe accounts set up to protect your expenses, what you do with the rest is personal choice. As long as that money is *extra* money—for lavish vacations or expensive gifts for grandkids—riding it out is still a viable option. The stock market is a bonus for you.

Leave the Monitoring to the Experts

Even if you're not relying on your stocks to pay the bills, I would advise consulting with someone you trust. You wouldn't try to contain a wildfire by yourself; you would leave that risky business to the professionals, especially after hearing my stories. Treat your finances the same way.

Monitoring is important in both firefighting and financial services. In firefighting, monitoring factors like wind speed, humidity, and temperature help predict fire behavior. Firefighting strategies will shift depending on the time of day and the environmental conditions. For example, during the intense heat and high wind speeds of midday, firefighters adopt cautious tactics to mitigate risks. But as the day progresses and temperatures cool down, a crew can be more assertive toward a less volatile fire.

Lookout observing the progress of a fire.

In financial services, a financial advisor who oversees your investments can serve as an early warning system for market downturns. An advisor can analyze various factors like national debt trends to predict market volatility. You can then shift investments into safer options or even transition them into cash to protect you from financial harm.

Prolonged exposure to fire hazards increases risk, and staying too long in volatile markets can lead to financial setbacks. You might not need that money, but I'm sure you want to keep it or grow it rather than lose it. In these cases, it's essential to have an expert watching your back.

After a significant market downturn, there's an opportunity to reassess strategies. Once market conditions stabilize, investors can take calculated risks or diversify portfolios to capitalize on potential market upswings. This strategic maneuvering allows you to still benefit from the market even in retirement.

As a financial advisor, I realize I'm biased, but I strongly believe that having an advisor monitoring your financial accounts is akin to monitoring a fire. It helps anticipate and prepare for heightened volatility so you have the best chance of success, especially when you factor in another risk: inflation.

Inflation

Inflation is the gradual uptick in prices of goods and services over time, which essentially means that the purchasing power of your money diminishes. Without getting into too much detail, inflation is triggered by the amount of dollars in circulation compared to the cost of goods and services. As the government prints more money, more dollars start chasing fewer goods. Consequently, it will cost more to buy the same amount of goods.

Inflation works much like a creeping fire in the forest; it erodes your buying power just as the flames erode the earth. If you don't plan for it, you can end up running out of money before you die.

Various factors affect inflation, such as increased demand or higher production costs. The US inflation rate has typically averaged 2.68 percent for the past twenty-four years.[15] During downturns it can go as high as 8 percent,[16] which was the 2022 inflation rate (possibly because of the post-pandemic supply chain crisis and other factors). While that 2.68 percent level of inflation is considered normal in a healthy economy, excessive inflation can pose challenges.

In a downturn, inflation starts to accelerate. It can reduce the value of savings and investments and impact overall economic stability. We saw that between 2021 and 2024 because in those three years, more dollars were chasing fewer goods, creating an inflation risk.

Most retired folks are on a fixed income and rely on pensions and Social Security for their retirement purposes. So when inflation rises, your plan gets messed up. That fixed amount of dollars you have to live on becomes less valuable. The dollar doesn't stretch as far because the cost of goods is increasing. People are suddenly confronted with the reality that their plan isn't going to work. They're drawing too much out because of the inflation, coupled with some market losses.

That's scary.

---

15   "Current US Inflation Rates: 2000–2024," US Inflation Calculator, accessed March 12, 2024, https://www.usinflationcalculator.com/inflation/current-inflation-rates.

16   "Current US Inflation Rates: 2000–2024," US Inflation Calculator.

I recently worked with a retired couple in their seventies. Before I started working with them, Mr. Garcia had a 401(k) with a company he retired from. He and his wife were drawing 4 percent from the account and using that to live on, in addition to Social Security money. But around 2021, when inflation took off, that planned withdrawal rate of 4 percent wasn't working. Mr. and Mrs. Garcia had to withdraw more than that out of their 401(k) simply to pay their bills. That got them worried because they were seeing the account drop at a faster clip. Their money wasn't going to last.

"We have to cut back," Mrs. Garcia told me. "We've been thinking about downsizing our house to get some extra money."

"Our car is on its last leg too," Mr. Garcia added, "but we're scared to buy a new one. We don't want to put the money into something that will lose value, if we can help it."

I was able to help the Garcias, as I'll explain in the next chapter. But this is a conversation I have all the time. You can save as much as you want, but when what you've saved is suddenly worth less, it's very stressful.

Seeking a Safe Haven

During the Taylor Park Fire, despite the intensity of the blaze surrounding us, my team found safety in a meadow. That was one of my first experiences with fire, and I definitely learned from it. I never forgot how quickly things can change.

Fire can be unpredictable, and so can markets and inflation. We know there will always be forest fires, and we know the market will always go up and down. It's how we learn to manage them that makes a difference. Every fire I worked was a learning experience that taught me fire management tactics, just like every experience with retirement planning teaches me to react and learn and plan some more.

Even experts have difficulty predicting the timing of the market. The Federal Reserve can decide to maintain or even lower interest rates while government spending remains high, creating a false sense of prosperity in the market. This can fool people into thinking that the markets are doing well when they're actually headed for another downturn. Likewise, when inflation shoots up, retirees may not be able to maintain their lifestyle. That's what is really driving the fear in my retiree clients—that their fixed incomes may not be enough. The market is unpredictable, and money isn't going as far as it used to.

The market and inflation are definitely going to continue to affect retirees. Fortunately, though, you can do something about it—you can proactively shield yourself from that blaze like my team did years ago. I'll tell you about it in the next chapter.

CHAPTER 3

FIREBREAK—SECURE INCOME STRATEGIES THAT LAST A LIFETIME

Fire burning up to a firebreak.

"That's the Marolf Ranch," I said as my team and I surveyed ominous black smoke billowing from the ponderosa pine of the Uncompahgre National Forest in the southwest part of Colorado. The fire was drawing closer and closer to a cluster of outbuildings on a homestead ranch that was probably more than a hundred years old.

"Sure is," said Dave G., the crew boss. "We better get moving. Let's get some backburning going so we can protect it."

I nodded enthusiastically, and my squad got moving. There were several ranches scattered throughout the forest, all about a mile apart from each other. We knew the ranchers personally because of work we had been doing felling trees to control a local beetle problem. The Marolfs had been kind enough to invite us over for dinner after we had spent the day marking trees to be felled near their home. There was no way we were going to let this fire, started by a lightning strike and now blazing through the huge forest, destroy their ranch.

"Lucky we did that backburn yesterday," Sarah, one of my crewmates, said as the charred fire line appeared before us next to the pasture road.

"No doubt about that," I said. The day before the fire was anticipated to reach the ranch, we took one of the pasture roads adjacent to the ranch and started a backburn. It was mostly grass for maybe fifty or a hundred yards, so we burned a long line parallel to the road all the way up to the forest.

We used a drip-fuel technique, where you run lines of a gas-diesel mix fluid along the road and burn up some of the surrounding material. This creates a strong barrier that, when the fire advances, leaves a substantial area of nothing to burn. My squad and I grabbed our fuel and poured small strips of fire up to eight feet wide parallel to the road. Then we started on the next section, maybe eight feet deeper, farther away from the road. That little eight-foot strip burned until it connected with the previously laid burn line.

As quickly as we could, the smell of smoke getting stronger and stronger, we built up that line. The burn location got eight or ten feet thicker each time we ran a strip through there. We did that for several strips until we got probably fifty to seventy-five yards wide, parallel to the actual ranch road. By midafternoon, the fire intensity had picked up and burned right up to our firebreak. There, as planned, it lost its intensity.

As the crew stood back on the safe side of the road, the Marolfs came out and approached us, arms waving, staring at the destruction across the way. "You deserve a medal, each and every one of you," Mrs. Marolf said. She pointed at our firebreak. "There's no way that fire can cross that."

Utilizing a forest road to create a firebreak.

And it didn't. We saved the Marolfs' home, along with all their outbuildings, corrals, and everything else on the homestead.

Now, let's flip this scenario around. What happens when the metaphorical fires of the market, inflation, and years and years of extended lifespan are raging toward your hard-earned retirement savings? You've got to create a metaphorical firebreak. That means not just protecting savings but actually generating income.

I'm not implying that you can't retire, but it's no longer about how big your pile of money is. If you have your funds in many types of retirement accounts, they're at risk, no matter what you do. You've learned that in the previous chapters. Therefore, you've got to shift away from the traditional approach of accumulating a lump sum and living off it a little at a time. Being proactive is key: You must take multiple steps to ensure your retirement savings aren't just shielded, but thriving.

If your financial firebreak is sturdy enough, your savings can not only survive but also generate income, even while the economy goes up in flames or the government increases withdrawal rate requirements. It doesn't get any better than that. In the previous chapters, you learned about all the different issues that can arise during a long retirement. Now it's time for solutions. In this chapter, we'll discuss the shelters you can put your money in to shield them from the flames.

Annuities: The Ultimate Firebreak

You've probably heard of pensions. Someone might have a pension from a large corporation, or if you're a retired government employee, you may have the ability to have a pension. You can use that pension in the planning process to determine your total income streams, including those from annuities, life insurance, or other pension plans.

Pensions work so well and are so desirable because they minimize potential losses during market downturns. You are guaranteed to keep receiving your income to pay your bills and maintain your lifestyle. The problem is that pensions are increasingly rare nowadays. So what do you do if you don't have one? You get an annuity.

Annuities are by far my favorite financial products for retirees. I sell them, and I use them myself. The retirement plan I came up with for my mom involves two annuities. Why do I love annuities so much? Annuities offer guaranteed lifetime income unaffected by outside factors, providing a stable output regardless of how long you live. Depending on how they are set up, annuities can provide guaranteed income or a safe haven for accumulation. Like a firebreak, an annuity removes the risk factor associated with playing the market. My mom is a perfect example of this. To hear this story in a more personal way and "meet" my mom and me, check out this video.[17]

I got my mom her first two annuities back in the late nineties, and she was making good interest. A few years later, in 2001, the market took a hit, plummeting by 30 to 40 percent for some folks. A lot of people lost a lot of money that year. At the time, my mom wasn't taking income from one of her annuities, but she called me up, somewhat miffed, when she got her statement.

"Al, I didn't earn any money in my annuity last year," she said.

"Yeah, Mom, that's great. You didn't lose a dime."

"But I didn't earn any interest."

---

17   https://www.youtube.com/watch?v=4f6t0PTk5Ug

"Talk to your friends at church." I laughed knowingly. At that time, she was going to the Catholic church in Northglenn, Colorado.

She paused. "Okay, son, I trust you," she finally said, and we started chatting about other things. After that she didn't mention anything at all about her annuity until the next year, when she called me up again.

"I got my statement from my annuity," she said.

"And?" I asked. "How did it look?"

"Hallelujah! I didn't lose a dime." We both laughed.

"You figured it out," I said. "A zero is far better than losing a good share of your money."

"All my friends at church were complaining about how much money they lost in their accounts last year," she said. "So, yes, I figured it out."

Fast forward to 2008. My mother was happy as a clam from 2003 all the way through 2007. She was earning good interest on her money in her annuities. Then the stock market took a colossal dive in 2008. My mom got her statement, and this time around, she already knew the drill.

"Hey, Al, I got my statement."

"How does it look?" I already knew the answer.

"Well, I didn't earn any interest," she said, "but when I was at church, I told all my friends they better get an annuity if they want to stop losing their money."

"What about all those referrals you sent my way?" I asked, smiling.

"They're sure glad they listened to me." My mom had become my advocate, referring people who were losing money in the markets. She went from being timid and uninformed about the system to telling her friends to "get ahold of my son because I'm not losing any money, and you are."

At the time of this writing, she's ninety-six. If you say anything negative about annuities to her, she'll give you a piece of her mind. Annuities have supported her for three decades now, so she's got good reason.

Pensions, interestingly, are another form of annuity. Some people may balk at that. In my case, as a federal employee and retired firefighter, I receive a pension from the government. Every year I receive a 1099 from the Office of Personnel Management that states "annuity pension." People may not realize it, but that pension is an annuity.

Amortization, Social Security, and the Lifetime Payment Annuity Model

People in retirement years like the idea of not having any risk. They can't afford to lose any money, in many cases. The idea of a potential lifetime payout without a pension can sound fishy. Most people don't understand this, but they do understand how their Social Security works.

If you've worked in the United States, you're probably expecting to receive Social Security at some point. These payments are not based on an interest rate. The payments that you receive from Social Security are mainly based on two factors: how much money you contributed in your lifetime, and your age at retirement. The government amortizes, or pays you regular payments, based on those factors.

For example, say you have X amount of money in your lifetime contributions for Social Security, and you're sixty-seven years old. The government knows that your life expectancy is around eighty-eight or eighty-nine, so based on that, they pay you a percentage of your total contributions. They create a formula that essentially amortizes, or pays you out, all the money you contributed based on your life expectancy. By the time your life expectancy is up, all the money that you contributed in your lifetime should have been paid back.

If you're still alive, you're still guaranteed to get that income until you die. If you die early, the Social Security program will keep your contribution money and use it to pay the people who outlived their money. They use it on the back end, taking the money from those who died and using it to pay those who outlived their money.

For annuities that offer lifetime payouts, insurance companies do the exact same thing. They have to calculate, based on certain actuarial tables, how long you're likely to live. They guarantee you a lifetime income based on your age at the time you start taking the income and how much money is in your account. They take those two factors and use a formula that says if you're sixty-seven years old, and you have a life expectancy of about eighty-eight years, they will amortize this money back out to you over that life expectancy time. If you're still alive, you still receive the payments until you pass away, and there is no money left over.

The Four Main Types of Annuities

When explaining the concept of annuities to my clients, I always tell them that there are hundreds of annuities, each with many different setup options. But it all boils down to four categories of annuities: pension annuities, variable annuities, fixed annuities, and fixed index annuities. There are agents who break it down even further or describe it in different ways, but I like to keep it simple.

The Pension Annuity

Most people understand how pensions work. A pension either pays you and your spouse for a set period of time or for a lifetime. There's no getting out of it. Once you pass away, that pension or that payment stops, and in most cases there are no beneficiaries; it's over. That's why I call the first type of annuity a *pension annuity*.

Technically, pension annuities are called *single premium immediate annuities*, and some people call them *deferred income annuities*. Whatever they're being called, though, this style of annuity works like a pension. It can't be changed once you buy it. You put your money into the insurance company, and it agrees to either start paying you right away or to defer payments for a few years.

There is the occasional exception. We could get into so many weeds here, but what I've described gives you the basic idea of the first type of annuity.

The Variable Annuity

Unlike a pension annuity, a variable annuity is a stock market–based product. The insurance company puts subaccounts into your contract that act like mutual funds. In most cases, they are mutual funds; therefore, they act like mutual funds. When the market goes up, you earn money; when the market goes down, you lose money. A variable annuity is an actual investment-grade product. The account value can quickly drop to zero because of stock market losses and your withdrawals.

A lot of people like this product, but I personally don't. Your money isn't safe. Some variable annuity products provide a payment for life—and supposedly the income for life is guaranteed—but the account can quickly go to zero because of stock market losses. Variable annuity products can also be complicated.

The Fixed Annuity

A fixed annuity is almost a mirror image of a certificate of deposit (CD) in a bank. A CD in a bank offers a set amount of interest for a period of time agreed upon in advance. With a fixed annuity, you have the same scenario, but from what I've seen over the years, a fixed annuity pays a bit more interest than CDs in banks over a similar time frame.

Here's the big difference between CDs and fixed annuities. With a CD in a bank, you have to claim any interest as ordinary income and pay taxes on it each year. A fixed-rate annuity is a tax-deferred product, which means you could leave it alone for the three- or five-year period and not pay any taxes until it matures. If the CD and the fixed-rate annuity paid the same interest at the end of the time frame, you would have more money in the fixed annuity because you've earned compound interest on top of compound interest. Some people call this *triple compounding*. One thing to note here is my description of a fixed annuity is for non-IRA accounts. An individual retirement account (IRA) defers the tax until you start withdrawing money from the account.

The Fixed Index Annuity

The fixed index annuity (FIA) seems to be the most popular, with the highest sales volume in the United

States currently.[18] For the most part, the FIA product operates like the fixed annuity. It is a guaranteed product, and it can provide lifetime income. With an FIA, you can take the income immediately or sometime down the road, depending on your individual retirement plan and when you start withdrawing.

The big difference between an FIA and a regular fixed annuity is the interest rate. The insurance company doesn't declare an upfront interest rate with an FIA. Instead, the interest rate depends on an index, and there are many indexes to choose from. A common one is the Standard and Poor's (S&P) 500. Interestingly, the insurance company doesn't actually invest your money in the underlying index, so you won't see a loss if the index goes down, but you do earn interest if the index goes up. Whichever index the insurance company is using, it agrees to give you part of the upside on an annual basis. So if the index goes up a percentage, you get part of that. On the flip side, indexed annuities don't directly participate in negative market years.

In an actual investment in the index itself, you earn the full upside, but you also take the full loss. If that index drops 20 or 30 percent, you lose money. In the indexed annuity, you've got a guaranteed floor that you can't lose

---

18 "LIMRA: US Annuity Sales Post Another Record Year in 2023," LIMRA, January 24, 2024, Accessed May 5, 2024, https://www. limra.com/en/newsroom/news-releases/2024/limra-u.s.-annuity-sales-post-another-record-year-in-2023/.

any money. This means you miss out on potential gains during good years, but at least you won't lose money if the index goes down. This is so powerful in practice, and my mom's experience exemplifies that.

Fixed Index Annuities: Where Does Your Money Go?

When I explain the fixed index annuity system to people, they're skeptical. It sounds too good to be true. They'll ask, "What is the insurance company doing with my money if it's not being invested in the index I'm earning interest from?"

The short answer is that the insurance companies are regulated. Primarily, they're required to put the majority of the money into long-term, grade-A corporate bonds. They are not allowed, by regulation, to invest the majority of your money in gold, oil, gas, and so on. Even though they're crediting you interest based on index performance, your money isn't being invested in that index. The majority of your money is in long-term, relatively safe investments that provide guaranteed interest earnings for the insurance company, regardless of what happens.

You may be wondering, if the money isn't being invested in the index that has a good year, how can the insurance company afford to pay interest that it hasn't received? What the insurance company is doing is recognizing that the average on any index is X amount, say 5 percent, using the S&P 500 as an example. So let's say the index has averaged 5 percent over the last twenty, thirty, or forty years, and the insurance company has promised to pay you a portion of whatever the index does. The company knows that in some years it might end up paying more than 5 percent in interest, and in some years it will pay less. On average, however, the index earns 5 percent, so the company is safe paying you that amount.

Annuity Laddering

You can go a step further with multiple annuities with a concept called *laddering*. Laddering is especially helpful to protect against long-term risks like inflation. Take another client of mine, Mrs. Smith, who had a high-flying IT job and a company match that allowed her to save up to $1 million dollars in her 401(k). She had a fairly high standard of living and needed $75,000 annually in retirement to continue her current lifestyle.

"Great," I said to her when she laid out her situation. "Let's take half a million dollars of your 401(k) and put it into an annuity that allows you to retire comfortably at seventy-five thousand dollars a year."

"Sounds good," she said, "but I've got a lot more than that. What about the rest of the 401(k)?"

"We have to address inflation. We can get you to the yearly seventy-five thousand dollars to retire on now with five hundred thousand dollars, so I suggest a laddering approach with most of the other half a million dollars. But first, let's set aside some emergency money. How much money do you have in your savings account or liquid somewhere outside your 401(k)?"

She looked down at her papers and shuffled through them. "I have about one hundred and fifty thousand dollars between my savings accounts, CDs, and investment portfolio."

"Terrific. In that case, we can use more of the second half-million for laddering. We could initiate three laddered annuities." I opened up my computer program to crunch the numbers, turning the monitor so she could follow along. "The average inflation rate as of now is 2.68 percent over the past three decades, but we can use 3 percent to make it a little conservative," I told her. "This calculator will project 3 percent inflation into the future. Let me reverse-engineer the process to determine the appropriate amount."

(Keep in mind that inflation fluctuates, but it historically works its way back to an average mentioned above.)

After taking a look at the projections, we set three annuities in motion, deferring them instead of immediately taking the income. Annuities work similarly to Social Security; if you delay when you start taking money out, the actual payout amount increases every year (more on that in a bit). With Mrs. Smith's first $500,000 annuity, she could launch into her retirement at $75,000 per year.

She understood the numbers but still had questions. "But let's say, in five or six or seven years, that seventy-five thousand dollars doesn't cover expenses anymore due to inflation. I'll have to cut back."

"You're right. If that happens, you can take one of those other annuities we set and start using it. So if, at age seventy-five, you start needing more income, we trigger one of these second annuities. That would provide you with a bump."

"How much of a bump?"

"Let's find out." I pulled up the annuity charts. Mrs. Smith would get another $15,000 a year if she started pulling from a second annuity at age seventy-five. Now she's up to $90,000 per year. Plus, she had a third annuity to deploy if she needed it. Between the three annuities, she could adjust for inflation and other increased expenses throughout the rest of her life.

By setting up more annuities, Mrs. Smith increased her protection against inflation with guaranteed incomes. We solved for inflation by kicking that money down the road and then collecting guaranteed incomes when those dollars get eaten up by inflation.

Firebreak Your Finances for Life

I likely scared you a little in chapters 1 and 2 with stories about inflation, withdrawal rates, extended retirement, and more. Sorry about that, but now that you've read chapter 3, I hope you're feeling a little better. Saving isn't enough, so instead, retirement is all about creating a reliable income. And, in my opinion, there's only a couple of ways to do that: annuities and life insurance.

There's so much risk out there, so you have to create a protective barrier around your assets. In firefighting, proactive measures are taken ahead of the fire's path, what's called a *firebreak*. The aim is to remove the fuel source, whether by cutting it down or conducting a controlled burn, or *backburn*. These measures effectively starve the fire, thereby protecting any ranches or homes that might be in its path.

A financial firebreak—creating stretches or zones with no fuel—means that when the fire or financial catastrophe reaches these areas, it can't sustain itself. That's what an annuity can do for your finances. Continued guaranteed income that will never run out erases the fear of running out of money before you die. You can get that guaranteed income through an annuity or life insurance, or even an old-fashioned pension, but annuities are most common.

Example of a backburn creating a firebreak.

Fixed index and lifetime payout annuities both offer a sustainable way to protect your retirement savings. During significant market downturns, your money remains protected within this product, shielded from the impact of market fluctuations. Even if you live to be 150 years old, that annuity will continue to pay for your lifestyle.

To set up an annuity, I suggest you contact a financial professional. Everybody's situation—or most people's, considering the endless number of situations that exist out there—will vary, and a professional can help you pick the setup that's right for you. The right annuity or annuities coupled with other income sources, like Social Security, offer a reliable foundation for a fulfilling retirement journey.

If you incorporate an annuity into your retirement plan, you can forget eating canned tuna and leaving the lights off. Whether it's enjoying a simple meal out or going on a dream vacation, there's no need to worry you'll run out of money if you live a long life. Instead, you can sit back, relax, and enjoy your hard-won retirement.

CHAPTER 4 ▌▬▬▬▬▬▬▬▬▬▬▬▬

OTHER INCOME STREAMS

"Listen up! We've got a campus full of students to save."

Our crew boss's bark immediately quieted the crew. I glanced toward nearby Pingree Park Forestry Camp, part of the Colorado State University campus in the Roosevelt National Forest, and shivered. I had gone there when I was a student, and as part of the summer camp, I had fond memories of roasting marshmallows and staying up late studying and laughing with my friends. Now named the "Hourglass Fire" for its irregular shape through the national forest, I was headed straight toward it. This one was personal.

"We're going to use several different approaches," Joe, our crew boss, said. "Number one, we've got some

D10 Caterpillars. Instead of using handlines, we're going to drive those bulldozers right through the forest to create a sixteen-foot fire line." I nodded. Those Caterpillars with sixteen-foot-wide blades were up to the job and would be much faster than a handline. "Number two, we'll form two handline crews to dig the spots where the bulldozers can't reach. And number three, we've got a few planes with slurry on their way that will dump directly on the fire."

With a combination of the dozers, the handlines, and slurry (a mixture of mostly water and fertilizer) to help suppress the fire's activity, I felt good about establishing a complete perimeter around my beloved camp. If it had been one or two methods, I would have been less confident. But with all three, I knew it would work.

As far as retirement goes, annuities provide that much-needed firebreak. But sometimes, one annuity—or even several—can use a boost. They aren't the only sources of regular income. We've already mentioned Social Security and pensions, but there are even more income streams you should be aware of. Don't think of them as separate; these various sources all come together when planning a retirement income strategy, and that's what this chapter is all about.

Life Insurance as an Income Stream

Annuities are an amazing option for secure retirement income, but they aren't your only option. Did you know that life insurance can function similarly to an annuity? Most people have a general idea of what life insurance is, but not how it works for people who are entering or nearing retirement. There are two types of life insurance, and most people usually only think of one. Let's go over both here.

Term Life Insurance

The type of life insurance you probably know about already is term life insurance. Term life insurance is a short-term plan often used earlier in life to protect assets. For example, if you're married and you have a term life insurance, if something happens to you, your spouse can pay off the mortgage and other debts.

The catch is that most term life policies, more than 80 percent of them, never pay any benefits.[19] The policyholder outlives the term of the policy. If you buy a fifteen-year term life insurance policy and pay monthly premiums, at the end of the fifteen years, the policy essentially expires.

---

19   Daniel A. Peters, Douglas A. McKay, "Life Insurance: Ownership and Investment Considerations," National Library of Medicine, *Plastic Surgery (Oakville, Ont.)*, v.22(1), (2014): 54–55. https://www.ncbi.nlm.nih.gov/pmc/articles/PMC4128435/.

Later in life, term life insurance can provide a tax-free benefit to heirs, children, or grandchildren upon the policyholder's death. Most people's debt decreases as they enter retirement, compared to when they were in their twenties, thirties, and forties, so heirs and beneficiaries can use the funds, not to pay off the mortgage on your house, but for other expenses that might be unrelated to your estate. However, if you outlive your policy, your payments still end up vanishing. None of this helps you fund your retirement, which brings us to the other type of life insurance.

Permanent Life Insurance

The second style of life insurance is permanent life insurance. Permanent life insurance comes in the format of whole life, universal life, and indexed universal life insurance. These different types of life insurance never go away, like term insurance. Once you set them up, as long as you pay the premiums, the policy can never be taken away from you, no matter how long you live.

Life insurance isn't like an annuity, where you receive a fixed amount monthly. Instead, you have the flexibility to withdraw the cash value at your preferred pace. But the faster you draw it out, the quicker it depletes. The only way to get that regular income stream is through an annuity because the annuity is guaranteed for as long as you live. Life insurance can complement this by offering additional funds, if needed, for various expenses. Setting up both is quite a common practice.

One considerable advantage to permanent life insurance is that all the interest earned on this reserve is tax-free, providing an advantage over annuities in terms of taxation. With non-IRA annuities, any interest earned is taxable when it is withdrawn, as it's considered gains.

Permanent life insurance is used more than term insurance in retirement because it can be used for a myriad of different purposes. Similar to term life insurance, permanent life insurance policies have a cost of insurance you have to pay monthly. You can, however, overfund the policy to use it like a bank account. If you pay more into it than the cost of the insurance policy, it starts to develop a cash reserve. That cash reserve can build and earn interest, exactly like any other financial instrument. Once you've built up that cash reserve, you can use it in different ways.

Some people use a life insurance cash reserve like their own lender. Rather than borrowing money from a bank to buy a car and paying interest to the bank, you might take the cash reserve from this policy and buy that same thing—a car or whatever—and then pay it back. But instead of paying a loan, you're replenishing your own reserves. The cash reserve can continue to grow, and this money is tax-free.

When you withdraw money, if you do pay it back, some policies with certain companies actually act as if that money never left. Let's say you take out $10,000 to buy something; the policy might continue earning interest as though the money is still there. As you pay it back, the account can then continue to increase in cash reserve.

If you have a policy with a lot of cash in it, you can take that cash out tax-free to supplement your income and lifestyle. You don't have to pay it back if you don't want to. Some people use that cash reserve for things like long-term care or medical bills. These life insurance policies also include special provisions that allow policyholders to use the death benefit to cover expenses associated with long-term care, such as nursing home costs. That's a huge deal for many retirees.

Real Estate

Now, let's go on to some other types of income. Rental properties are popular among older individuals. I personally own rental properties. They are a common investment choice as people age, providing a steady stream of income built into their financial strategy.

The issue I run into is when somebody counts solely on rental properties for their retirement nest egg. "I've got plenty of retirement money with these rentals," they might tell me. "I don't need an annuity." Well, rentals can be fickle, and although a good source of income, they aren't a guaranteed source. When they're working, you can make some good, steady cash flow. But all too often, rentals have issues. I have several real-world examples to share with you.

First, there's the possibility of not receiving rent. I have a client named Chuck, a terrific guy with a heart of gold. He's seventy years old and owns twenty rentals. He makes a boatload of money. I was talking to him one day, and he told me he was having problems with a renter.

"The lady told me, 'I lost my job. I can't pay you,'" he said, shrugging. "I didn't want to kick her out, so I told her to go ahead and pay me when she could."

Six months later, we had another appointment to discuss his investments. "Whatever happened to that renter you were having issues with?" I asked. "Did you get things sorted out?"

Chuck groaned. "Still haven't gotten a dime. The renter is still there, and I'm still paying the taxes and utilities, of course. Losing money."

Second, there's the possibility of issues with the actual property. The tenant lets a sink overflow, and it floods the house. All of a sudden your renter has to move out while you upgrade, replace, and remodel. During that time, you're not making any income. I recently had a client who came to my office because of a problem like this.

"I need money out of my annuity," she told me.

"What happened, Tanya?"

"My renter had a small kitchen fire. It didn't damage a lot, but the issue was the fire department. When they came in, they hosed everything down and flooded the place. I have to redo my entire kitchen."

"That's awful," I said. "How much do you think you need?"

Tanya looked worried. "I'm honestly not sure. I think it will be anywhere from fifteen thousand dollars to thirty thousand dollars based on the quotes I've gotten."

I nodded, and we looked at each other. We both knew that while she was spending that money, she would also not be making any income from an empty rental.

You may be thinking, "Isn't there some kind of insurance to cover stuff like that?" Of course. I have renter's insurance on both my rentals, a home and a condo. But even that doesn't make a rental a safe source of retirement income—you're not receiving rent if any issues crop up.

I actually experienced this myself not too long ago. My condo is on the second floor of a three-story building. Lo and behold, one day the renter called and said, "The ceiling's got a huge bulge in it. Something's happening."

"That's no good. I'll get the maintenance people out there tomorrow," I said.

At ten o'clock that night, she called me again. "Oh my God! There's water pouring in from the ceiling."

"Great," I said. I had to send over an emergency maintenance call, and obviously my renter had to move out. The next morning I called the homeowners association (HOA). The representative said, "No fault of yours. We'll come in, rip out the ceiling, and fix those pipes."

Over the course of a month, the HOA sent people in to fix the pipes. But when I checked in with the repair people, they told me, "There's a lot of water damage all over the rental. The HOA replaced the direct damage, but the water got everywhere, including the walls and the floor. We have to contend with the possibility of mold."

It was time to call the insurance company and explain the situation.

"We would be happy to assist you," the representative told me. "You just have to pay your deductible."

I had forgotten about that. "How much is it?"

"Two thousand dollars."

Oh, wow. I had to come up with the first $2,000 before the insurance company stepped in. The repair people did their work and fixed it all up. Finally, two to three months later, I put a renter back in there. But how much money did I lose? I lost my deductible, and I lost a couple of months' worth of rent. If I had been depending on that rent, I would have been in trouble.

Hopefully you can see why you shouldn't count on a rental property as your main source of guaranteed income. Rent can go away at the drop of a hat, or it can even cost you money instead of making you money for a period of time.

Oil Rights

Oil rights aren't something I encounter a lot, but some situations have come up. Pockets of oil or natural gas have accumulated over millions of years all over this country. If you travel the countryside, especially in the Midwest, you'll see tons of oil derricks moving up and down, sucking oil or natural gas out of the earth.

Not every landowner has the resources for oil or natural gas extraction, not to mention enough land to install these derricks and try to access oil or natural gas. But, if you own land and you're in the right spot, this is a real opportunity for income. Let's say you have forty acres of land in Wyoming. You own the natural resource rights to that land. An oil company representative comes to you and says, "We have a high suspicion that we could access some natural gas, oil, or some other mineral on your land." The company creates a contract specifying what the exploration company is looking to do, including mitigations for cleanup and other related matters.

If you agree to the terms and the company decides to drill for natural gas, it will give you a part of the profits.

As long as the company is extracting this resource, you, as a landowner, get an income from that. It's an ongoing stream of income for as long as the gas lasts.

In large areas like Texas, Oklahoma, and other places with expansive tracts of land, companies can also set up fracking. They create one drill site, and then they can reach out in many different directions to extract the resources. The drill site may not be on your land, but you still get a part of the income if you own natural resource rights.

Oil rights or natural gas drill sites can produce income for a landowner, and those drill sites or drill rights can be passed on from generation to generation. The only downside is if the resource dries up. At that point, the company caps the drill site, and your income stops. In some cases, the resource that's in the ground lasts for many years; in others, it doesn't last long. No one can really tell until it happens.

What to Do If You Don't Have Enough

The other day, a local woman named Kathy called me asking for help.

"I want to sell my house," she told me. "I hurt my back, and I can't work. I'm sixty-five years old, and I'm on SSDI. I'm going to sell my house and move to Portland to be closer to my daughter."

"Okay," I said. "How much are you expecting to get from the sale of your home?"

"I still owe on the mortgage," she said. "I think I should get around one hundred and fifty thousand dollars. And if I make too much money, they'll take away my SSDI."

"Do you have retirement savings or other assets?"

"No," she said. This woman was expecting to move to an expensive neighborhood and retire with only $150,000 and her Social Security Disability Insurance payments. Ultimately, I had to tell her it wasn't possible.

I run into this a lot. There are times when I can't help people because they don't have enough money. Many retirement experts recommend between $1 million and $1.5 million for retirement savings. The demographics I have here in Colorado show most people have a 401(k) with amounts like $219,000 or $174,000. I would say my average client has anywhere from $100,000 to $350,000. Is that enough to retire on? Maybe, but it gets real difficult.

Disability Programs and Part-Time Work

Part-time work doesn't affect your Social Security eligibility or benefits. Social Security is not a means-tested program. Your lifetime contributions and the age at which you begin receiving them determine your benefits. Part-time work also doesn't affect pensions, annuities, rental income, or royalties from oil rights—each of these income sources operates independently.

The only scenario in which part-time work affects you is if you're enrolled in means-tested programs like disability, Medicare, or Medicaid. In such cases, part-time work may impact your eligibility.

Kathy, mentioned earlier, is an example of someone on means-tested programs. She wanted to sell her house for $150,000 and move to Portland and live with her daughter. She didn't want the $150,000 to affect her SSDI. But because SSDI is a means-tested program, if you make more than a certain amount in other sources, it disqualifies you from disability. This money can be from a part-time job, selling a home, or any other income stream. If you put that money into an annuity, it would show up as income for you, and that could wreck any means-tested benefits.

When a Lot Isn't Enough

Sometimes even that million dollars isn't enough. Take the example of Mr. Edwards, a client of mine who lives in a suburb of Denver. He owns a million-dollar house, and he was used to making $150,000 a year as a marketing manager. He belonged to an expensive country club and frequently traveled internationally. When he started thinking about an early retirement, we sat down and looked at his savings.

"I've got my 401(k), four hundred and fifty thousand dollars, and my Social Security," he said.

"No pension?"

"No, but I've got Social Security."

I reviewed his lifestyle and expenses, then turned toward him. "I'll be honest with you. You can't continue to live your same lifestyle when you retire. You'll need to downsize and cut some corners."

Mr. Edwards, completely blindsided, reiterated his earlier accounting: "I have four hundred and fifty thousand dollars in my 401(k). That should be plenty."

"It's enough to retire on, but not enough to retire on while maintaining your lifestyle. If you retire at sixty-two years old, it won't be enough because you've got twenty-five years or more of life expectancy." He gave me this blank look, so I decided to break it down. "Okay, your house and vehicles are paid off. What's your desired income to pay for everything else?"

"I would say around eighty thousand dollars a year to live comfortably."

"How much is your Social Security? What other incomes do you have?"

"I'll get twenty-three thousand dollars per year from Social Security if I retire early, and I have a rental property too. It nets me a thousand dollars a month."

"Perfect. We'll count that as income." We added those two numbers together to get $35,000. That put us

$45,000 short of his annual goal. "Let's plug the amount of your 401(k) into this formula and see how much income we can get through an annuity." The formula is based on factors like age and amount deposited. When I ran the numbers, we found that he could get $30,000 if he retired at age sixty-two. With that $30,000 and the rest of his income, we were up to $65,000.

This meant I had the dubious honor of telling him, "Mr. Edwards, you haven't saved enough money to have an eighty-thousand-dollar-per-year lifestyle and retire early. I mean, I can help you almost get there, but I can't get you all the way. And keep in mind that this is today's dollar we're talking about. None of this is inflation adjusted."

He finally understood. "So how do we solve this?" he asked gruffly.

"One option is for you to work a couple more years to grow that 401(k)," I said. "You could also go ahead and retire on your sixty-five-thousand-dollar guaranteed income from those three sources. If you want to keep going on all these expensive golfing trips and living in that big house, maybe you can take some consulting work on the side."

Making Your Firebreak

People are living longer, which means our retirement savings are expected to stretch for many more years.

And with the 4 percent withdrawal rule debunked and markets wavering, what are we supposed to do? Like I mentioned earlier in the example of the unfortunate Mr. Jones, a 401(k) isn't really an income stream. It's an unprotected pile of money at risk of burning up. So in addition to those annuities or even an annuity ladder, it's good to look into other sources of income.

With a plan of attack that involves firebreaks, handlines, and slurry, a team of firefighters can stop even a huge fire in its tracks. Likewise, if you can add income from real estate, oil rights, life insurance income, or other forms of regular cash flow to your retirement plan, you'll be ready to fight off a recession, inflation, or whatever else comes your way. Even if you don't have enough now, or whether you have a little or a lot in your retirement savings, there are steps you can take to get some of that lifetime income and work your way toward a secure retirement. Lifelong income, not savings, is the key to securing your financial future in retirement, and multiple streams of income can help you live not only safely but comfortably and enjoyably.

CHAPTER 5

TAXATION TACTICS—QUENCHING THE FINANCIAL FLAMES

Slurry drop.

Slurry drop to limit the fire's progress.

One of the fire tactics employed to manage a fire—not to extinguish it, but to slow its progression or guide it into a specific area—is the use of a fire retardant known as slurry. I briefly mentioned slurry in the last chapter. A mixture of mostly water and fertilizer, slurry was designed to protect trees, homes, and other structures from going up in flames. The compound, artificially colored with red dye so firefighters can see it on the ground, coats trees and vegetation to provide insulation against an approaching fire.

We decided to use slurry on a firefighting mission in a national forest in the southwest corner of Colorado. The fire had expanded and consumed several homes, including those of ranchers, along with their barns and other outbuildings. Fire officials were concerned that the fire was going to continue.

The fire was heading toward a major ranch and all its outbuildings. We used bulldozers to dig a fire line through the forest, but as we got into the heavy timber—ponderosa pine, very thick and tall—the fire started to intensify. The winds picked up as predicted. We were in the middle of the forest, and the flames reached a point where the fire line was no longer going to be effective.

For our safety, we had to backtrack to get out of the path of the fire. As we moved back down the line to a safety zone, we directed one of the slurry bombers to come in and lay a line of slurry on the path we were on, to keep the fire from trapping us. A little about the slurry bombers: The bombers were these mammoth tankers that were mostly from World War II and specially designed to withstand the flex that occurs when an airplane drops a considerable amount of weight in the air. This flex significantly affects the wings and body of the aircraft. Planes today aren't built with that same structure; they're much lighter because they don't have to drop large payloads of weight. That's why we had to use these older planes that have the structure to do that.

The slurry bomber that came flying up over the fire was a PB4Y-2, characterized by its glass nose that typically housed a gunner. The slurry, two thousand gallons of red goo, poured out of the belly of this thing in a staggering mist. We watched the stuff fall right down the line where we were, and braced ourselves for impact. It practically knocked us to the ground, and in the end, we were covered in slime. It was unpleasant, but it saved our lives. The damper on the fire in that immediate area allowed us to continue down the path to safety. We made fun of each other's slime-monster looks and got a good laugh.

Time for the financial connection here: taxes. This chapter is all about tax management for those nearing retirement. If taxation creeps up on you, it can spiral out of control and become unmanageable. In some cases, drastic measures have to be taken to keep a lot of your assets from going up in smoke. To address these fiscal challenges head-on, you've got to get a grip on the retirement tax scene. Assuming you've got your income streams set up, here's what you can do to take advantage of tax breaks, ease your tax load, and keep your finances protected in the long run.

Understanding the Tax Landscape in Retirement

When you're in the throes of your working years, you think about taxes in one way. When you're approaching retirement, you think about them in a different way. But what is that transition, and what are those differences?

During their regular career years, people understand that there's a certain tax rate, and they may not like that tax rate. When they stop working, people tend to think they'll fall into a lower tax bracket because they won't make as much money. That's why they don't see an IRA as an issue. IRAs are taxable when you start to draw out of them during retirement years, and this can affect how much money you have.

Traditional IRAs also come with required minimum distributions (RMDs). With a traditional IRA, you must take your distributions because the government wants you to pay tax on those distributions. So even if you don't need the money, it has to come out of the IRA, you have to pay the tax, and then you have to figure out what to do with that money. Refer to the section on qualified charitable distributions later in this chapter for more details on this topic.

In addition to that, traditional IRA money hasn't been taxed yet, so the government actually owns a sizable chunk of whatever is in there. People often forget that they don't own the full amount they have in the bank, and that can lead to problems if they're counting on that full amount. For example, let's say you're in a 20 percent tax bracket and have $100,000 in an IRA. If you pull it all out, you only have $80,000. That's a problem that people don't consider as they're saving money throughout their career. It's only when they get ready to retire that they realize they owe the government a handsome piece of their IRA.

Finally, another problem separate from the IRA is that tax rates have been going up in many areas at local, state, and county levels. I live in Colorado, and city taxes are rising here. We also had a big jump in our property taxes. My taxes on my personal home almost doubled between 2023 and 2024.

People don't factor these taxes into their retirement plans. Once you get into retirement years on a fixed income, this can present a problem. What if, all of a sudden, your property taxes go way up? That will really take a bite out of regular ordinary living income and can have a detrimental effect on the spendable money you have for eating out, taking a vacation, or buying a new car.

Roth Rollovers

So the question is, How can you leverage tax deductions to protect you in retirement? This is a hard one because tax deductions traditionally favor free enterprise. The tax deductions you're allowed to have when you're working for a corporation are limited. Many people leverage tax deductions by creating a small business, but that's outside the purview of this book.

One of the most cost-effective ways to leverage those deductions is to plan for taxes before retirement. Roth IRA conversions are one way to do this. Roth IRA conversions involve creating a Roth IRA and moving money from your traditional IRA to your Roth IRA. You convert this money to the Roth IRA until it's all in the Roth IRA.

When you do this, two things happen. First, you're paying taxes at a faster rate. Second, once you reach retirement age and follow the IRS guidelines, all the money you draw out in retirement is tax-free. The other nice thing about Roth IRAs is no required minimum distribution, because the government already got their taxes. Therefore, if you don't need the money, you can keep it right in that account.

Paying taxes ahead of time in a Roth IRA leverages a concept created back in the nineties. It allows you to convert money at or before reaching retirement age. Then, when you're in retirement, you've got tax-free money.

Roth Rules

IRS guidelines state that the Roth IRA must be in place for five years, and you must be over the age of fifty-nine and a half before you can draw money out tax-free. The most important thing people can do is make that Roth account at least five years before retirement.

If you have a 401(k) through your current employer, and you're under the age of fifty-nine and a half, you can't do a Roth rollover. You cannot move that money to anywhere else; you can't move it out of the 401(k). Some 401(k) accounts, however, now allow you to start a Roth IRA alongside your regular 401(k).

The IRS also has another rule called a *forever clock*. Let's say you put $500 into a Roth IRA, whether it's a bank account, annuity, or mutual fund. Even if that account is gone twenty years later—maybe you spent it or had to cash it out—you have already started the five-year clock. It starts when you open the Roth account, regardless of whether that new account is still in existence or not. So if you put money into some type of Roth IRA when you're sixty, you don't have to wait five years; you've already met the five years.

What If I'm Already Retired?

A Roth conversion can be challenging once you're retired because many people are on a fixed income. Even in retirement, however, some people have the financial ability to do conversions. I've had clients with a large IRA, Social Security, a pension, some oil rights, and other forms of income like rental properties. Folks like that have enough income to live on, but they still have those RMDs from their IRA. A Roth conversion can help them accelerate that process and put the money somewhere where it can grow tax-free.

This strategy essentially lets you get ahead of the curve, or financially get ahead of this requirement. There are a couple of specific exclusions. I won't get into them here, since exclusions don't pertain to most people; they usually apply to those who make a lot of money. The IRS has many rules regarding Roth accounts, so anyone looking to do this should consult their tax advisor.

Tax Bracket Considerations for Roth Conversions

When you do that Roth conversion, you can space it out so you don't end up with a huge tax bill in a single tax year. That's where your tax bracket comes in. For example, let's say somebody makes $100,000 a year, putting them in the 22 percent tax bracket, the tax bracket for joint married filers, currently ranging from $82,000 to $182,000. If you're starting a Roth conversion and making $100,000 per year, you have about an $82,000 window for your conversion before you get put into the next tax bracket.[20]

So what do we do? We strategize and take advantage of the room left in that tax bracket. This is part of what I do as a retirement planner. These are strategies that I

20   "IRS Provides Tax Inflation Adjustments for Tax Year 2024," Internal Revenue Service, November 9, 2023, Accessed April 12, 2024, https://www.irs.gov/newsroom/irs-provides-tax-inflation-adjustments-for-tax-year-2024.

help people build so they don't increase their tax rate by doing Roth conversions. Somebody making $150,000 a year only has a $41,950 window to convert to Roth money before they move into another tax bracket.

Some people have the financial means and don't care about entering another tax bracket because they make enough money or their situation is specific. But most people don't want to go into the next tax bracket, and for them, a financial advisor can plan a conversion schedule that keeps them in their current bracket.

What Does This Have to Do with Annuities?
Putting Your Roth IRA to Work

What is the connection between annuities and Roth conversion? In a nutshell, you can use a Roth IRA to fund an annuity. A Roth can be placed anywhere you choose—whether it's in a mutual fund, a bank account, or an annuity.

First, let's revisit Roth IRA money as it is defined. A Roth IRA is taxed before the money goes into the account. So let's say you have an IRA, and you've decided to move that IRA over to a Roth IRA. A Roth IRA can take many forms. Let's say you choose a Roth IRA bank account. If your name is "Rose Smith," your bank statement will say something like "Rose Smith Roth IRA account." You have paid the tax. Everybody knows, including the IRS, that you paid. That's why it's designated as a Roth.

Now we can engage in conversations about where to put this money. One option is a Roth IRA annuity. The concept behind putting your money into a Roth IRA annuity is straightforward. That Roth IRA annuity can provide income for life, similar to other annuities we've discussed. The difference arises when you begin withdrawing income from this Roth annuity. It's tax-free money until your passing, with no further tax obligations.

Suppose you're sixty years old, and you've converted your 401(k) over into a Roth IRA annuity from which you will draw your retirement income. Maybe you're in the 22 percent tax bracket; you've permanently eliminated that 22 percent tax on your money by paying your taxes in advance.

This differs from having the Roth in a portfolio, such as a mutual fund. In a case like that, there is no guaranteed income. It's a pile of tax-free money, sure, but it's still just a pile of money. Drawing out money to live on could potentially deplete the tax-free funds if withdrawn too quickly or if the fund loses value. And what if you pass away prematurely and have named your child as the beneficiary? They won't receive the income, but they will inherit the money tax-free.

I hope you can now see why Roth money holds remarkable value in an annuity. You do, however, have to

meet the two provisions I mentioned earlier to qualify
for a Roth IRA annuity income: being over the age of
fifty-nine and a half before initiating withdrawals, and
the money being held for at least five years before initiating withdrawals.

For instance, suppose you're fifty-five years old and
you begin a Roth, conducting conversions along the way.
Once initiated, the five-year clock starts ticking. When
you reach sixty years old, having converted all your IRA
into Roth funds during that time, you possess $450,000
that you have converted. When you start withdrawing
income, as mentioned earlier, it remains tax-free rather
than being subject to a 22 percent tax rate.

Self-Directed Roth IRA and Mandatory Distributions

Another aspect that people don't often account for is
the self-directed IRA. Many people have embraced this
strategy. You take money out of your IRA account and
use it to invest in assets like real estate, such as rental
properties. It can be a store, a house, an apartment,
anything. And once it's in place, you can collect rent
from it. You've self-directed this IRA money out of a
plan, an IRA somewhere, into a piece of property.

It's a tempting prospect if you're under retirement
age, especially because you're not taking any money out
of your cash flow. The assets still count as part of your
IRA. Be aware, though, of the mandatory distribution

requirement, which, at the time of writing, kicks in at age seventy-three. If your IRA doesn't have enough liquid assets to cover the mandated minimum distribution, you'll be forced to sell off that property to comply with IRS rules. Many people fail to factor this in, and it catches them by surprise.

This is a potential drawback of self-directed IRAs invested in real estate, especially as individuals approach the age of seventy-three, where mandatory distributions become necessary. You might find yourself needing to convert property assets back into liquid funds to meet IRS obligations of RMDs.

The IRS says it's legal, and people do it. Unfortunately, some folks do it without understanding that at some point in time, they're going to have to start liquidating.

Roth IRAs and Annuity Planning for Younger Folks

Most of you reading this book are nearing retirement. But if you're wondering about your kids or grandkids, I want to tell you a little about annuities for younger folks. Yes, they are an option, and a good one at that.

I started working with a thirty-eight-year-old woman named Stephanie. She had a 401(k) from a previous employer with $80,000 in it.

"Should I roll the old 401(k) into my new company 401(k)?" she asked me.

"Absolutely not."

She laughed. "Then what would you recommend?"

"Take that old 401(k) money and move it to a Roth IRA," I said. "You'll need to pay taxes on it now, but it will be tax-free when you retire."

"Okay," she said, sounding uncertain. "That seems like a lot of taxes to pay now."

She was right. If we took that whole 401(k) and rolled it over into a Roth in a single year, she would have had $80,000 worth of income to show Uncle Sam in one year. That would have bumped her up to another tax bracket, and we didn't want to do that. We looked at her income and the tax brackets and did some math.

"Based on your income and expenses," I said, "if you take ten thousand dollars of that money and convert it to Roth each year, you won't go up to the next tax bracket. You'll pay the taxes on the extra ten thousand dollars annually. You do that for eight years in a row, and at age forty-six, all the money has been converted to a Roth IRA. Because you're paying the taxes on it a little at a time, it won't impact your life very much at all."

The next question was what type of Roth IRA account to use. If you're younger, you have a lot of options here. You want to put it in a mutual fund? Great. God bless you. You want to put it in a bank account and earn 3 percent? Do it. You want to put it in an annuity? There's a way to do that too.

After talking to Stephanie about her goals, we came up with a solid plan for her. Since she's young, she decided to use a deferred income annuity using a Roth IRA. This type of account isn't designed for immediate income, and there are no fees or charges. It functions like a bank account and will grow without any risk of loss until she reaches age fifty-nine and a half. At that point, she'll have an ample amount of money in this account, and it will all be tax-free because she converted it to Roth.

That's how a younger person can take advantage of this tax-savings rule. An annuity is an absolute gold mine for someone who wants tax-free income for life, and you can plan for that early. If you're in a 22 percent tax bracket when you retire, and you've done a Roth IRA annuity conversion, you're essentially saving 22 percent of your money every single year because it's not being taxed anymore. This is especially true if tax rates go up. What do you think tax rates will be in the future?

Qualified Charitable Distributions for Excess Funds

Once you're past the age of seventy-three and in retirement, you have to take the RMD from your IRAs, 401(k), 403(b), and all those other pretax accounts. But what if you don't need that money to live on? If you didn't do that Roth rollover but still want to get a tax benefit, there's another option. The IRS allows people who have the means and already have enough income to do a qualified charitable distribution (QCD).

A QCD is where you can take your RMD and send it directly to a charity. If you do that, then the tax on that withdrawal isn't applied. Essentially, you're sending it to the charity tax-free. Current IRS rules state that you can do that with as much as $100,000 in any given year. I have some clients who are extremely wealthy, and we leverage QCDs quite a bit.

Slurry Bombs and Uncle Sam

Since about the mid-1980s, tax rates have been pretty steady in the United States. But we live in an uncertain world—one where the winds can change and a fire can quickly spread. You have to be ready to dump a load of fire retardant to protect yourself. To be able to do that, of course, you've got to plan ahead and have those World War II bombers full of lifesaving, fire-stopping slurry.

Not everyone remembers to do that kind of planning. Once they retire, so many people realize that taxation depletes their ability to sustain their lifestyle. Folks don't fully understand this until it's happening to them. That is, they don't understand unless someone warns them to build that slurry into their retirement plan.

Through the topics of this chapter, we've explored some ways to avoid undue taxation during retirement. Roth conversions are best for this, especially for those who aren't yet in retirement. I work with many of my clients to schedule rollovers to an IRA annuity first, which helps people avoid any future losses and fees. Then, systematically over the next several years, you convert the IRA a little at a time to Roth, paying the tax as you go. At the end of the period, when you've converted all the IRA to Roth, you wait until you're fifty-nine and a half. Assuming the IRA is in an annuity, you have tax-free income for life. If you're already sixty, you have to delay taking the income for five years.

For people who have already retired, Roth rollovers or conversions still aren't out of the question. Instead, this is an attractive strategy for getting ahead of a tax time bomb. On the other side of the equation, younger folks can schedule rollovers and leverage annuities to get ahead of their retirement planning and ensure a tax-free retirement. That's exactly what my client Stephanie did.

What about people who have a lot of wiggle room in their budgets? Don't forget about those QCDs. Instead of having to take out money required by the IRS, you can choose to set up a QCD to send that money to a charity without paying taxes on it. Whether you're using a Roth IRA annuity or QCDs, make sure to load up your plane with slurry. If you plan ahead, you can ensure that your funds are protected from the raging fires of rising taxes during retirement.

CHAPTER 6

LONG-TERM CARE PREPAREDNESS— BATTLING THE UNEXPECTED BLAZE

Fire intensely burning underbrush.

In the nineties, I was on the Crooked Creek Fire in Alaska. It was up on the Kenai Peninsula near the humongous Tustumena Lake. I was assigned to scout out fires with two other guys, Jay and Brad, way out in the bush. Our little camp was far from any civilization; we were on our own. Sometimes our two-way radios worked and sometimes they didn't because we were too far away from base camp.

We needed to be this far out because fires in Alaska are unique. Once a fire reaches into the tundra, the embers can stay alive for a couple of years. Yes, *years*. They remain alive under the tundra, even through the winter, because they stay insulated under the surface. When summer comes, these fires pop up in different places. We were assigned to find some fires that would smoke, then disappear underground for a time.

A few days into our search for these elusive fires, our trio came across a small dip in the ground's surface, maybe a quarter of an acre in size, with trees all around. In the dip were some logs that had obviously been tipped over, dragged, and torn apart not too long ago. We looked at each other nervously. A gust of air blew, and we knew for sure—a grizzly was close. We could smell it.

To search for grubs and worms, grizzly bears rip apart trees and dive into the rotting, stinking debris. Their oil glands produce a musk that smells a little like a skunk, but the bears are obviously far more dangerous. A grizzly bear's odor is overpowering and unpleasant.

It was quiet—eerily quiet—in that little valley surrounded by forest. The hair on the back of my neck stood up. *This bear is probably watching us*, I thought. *Oh, God.* I grasped my Pulaski.

"Let's get out of here," Jay muttered. Brad and I nodded. As swiftly and quietly as we could, we hightailed it out of there over the rough terrain, jumping across logs and limbs. I got ready to leap over a log in front of me and ensured my axe blade was pointed down. Planting my free hand on the log, I hurtled over it and flung my legs out. One leg flew right into my blade.

I hissed as the axe sliced above my knee, cutting through my quad. My pant leg grew red with blood, and I knew immediately that I would need stitches. Then, the first few raindrops hit. There was no sense in trying to look for fires now that it was raining; they wouldn't pop up anymore. We were done for the day, but we still had to put some space between us and the bear. We hurried back to our tents.

"Hang on," I said after a few minutes. My leg was bleeding like crazy. I wrapped my handkerchief around the wound to try to stop the bleeding.

"Geez, Al, what did you do?" Jay asked.

"Hit my axe." I grimaced as I tightened my makeshift tourniquet. "Let's go."

I was able to limp along through what quickly became a downpour. By the time we reached our tents, it was dark. I wasn't near any first aid; I had to deal with this on my own. There was nothing my partners could do.

I climbed into my tent, which was soaking wet because we had had to set up camp on the tundra. As I sat in there trying to work on my leg, the tent started to fill with water. There was no high ground, no place to stay dry. My sleeping bag was a soggy mess, like everything else. With my headlamp, I saw that the blood was still flowing, and I couldn't stop it no matter how much compression and gauze I used. I was getting nervous. It was maybe midnight or one o'clock, and I was exhausted. But I was terrified of going to sleep; I could bleed out. *Oh, God. What have I gotten myself into here?*

I stayed awake all night. By the time morning came, the bleeding had slowed and was merely oozing now. I didn't have anything dry to wrap my leg with, so I had to tough it out. As the sun rose, Brad, Jay, and I crawled out of our tents. My fellows took one look at me and frowned.

"You're not in any shape to keep going," Brad said. "Let's tear down and hike out." With my leg still dripping, we hiked an unpleasant fourteen miles back to the little town of Ninilchik, where we could get picked up and taken to the fire camp at the local high school.

Obviously, I didn't die that day. But the reason I'm sharing this story is that we don't know when our health might take a turn. Something, whether a car accident, a heart attack, or a Pulaski, could either end our lives or severely hamper us. Having a long-term care plan is important because you need to prepare for the unexpected. A lot of people don't plan for this at all, while others take out a long-term care policy. In this chapter, we'll go over some of the aspects of long-term care planning, and I'll present another option to ensure your needs are met, no matter what happens.

The Three Phases of Retirement

In the world of long-term care, people talk about three phases of retirement. The first phase is the "Go-Go Years." You're maybe in your sixties or early seventies, traveling, playing pickleball, doing all sorts of activities, and you go, go, go.

After the Go-Go Years, you enter the "Slow-Go Years" of your life. You still want to keep doing those fast-paced activities, but your energy level and your physical capacity to maintain that pace isn't there. The Go-Go Years can quickly turn into Slow-Go Years. Countless people blow out their knees playing pickleball, mess up their shoulders playing tennis, or fall off their bike while mountain biking, for example. After you get through these Slow-Go Years, you get into the "No-Go Years." At this point, you don't have the ability to do much anymore.

Financially speaking, if you don't plan for the Slow-Go and No-Go Years, you're heading for disaster. Long-term care encompasses a variety of potential events, and you never know when those Slow-Go Years will hit. For instance, people sometimes unexpectedly experience a stroke either in retirement or as they're preparing for retirement. This can severely impact their quality of life and change the trajectory of their retirement.

This is exactly what happened to a nice couple I worked with, the Williams, who lived out in eastern Colorado. Mr. Williams was a grain mill inspector, and Mrs. Williams had been a homemaker for many years. I helped them create a retirement plan with a target date of four or five years. Two years after we started this, and with another two years to go before Mr. Williams was going to retire, Mrs. Williams called me in tears.

"My husband had a stroke," she told me. "He was on the job, and the stroke put him in a bed. He's here at the house. It's been several weeks, and he can't move one side of his body."

Slowly, I gathered the details. There was no way Mr. Williams could continue working. Since this wasn't necessarily a work-related accident, he wouldn't qualify for workers' compensation. Mrs. Williams was stranded. On top of that, Mr. Williams was a big guy, and his wife was petite. She couldn't get him into the bathroom or help him take a shower. Caretakers would have to help with those tasks, and that would be expensive.

"We don't have a plan for this," Mrs. Williams said to me after she laid out the situation. "What do we do?"

I'll tell you what we did a bit later. You can see through this story, though, how fast circumstances can change. The Williams had a comfortable lifestyle, and all that came to an end in a couple of days without any warning. There was no way to predict it, and things like this happen every day.

Traditional Methods of Long-Term Care Planning

Anything could happen along those three phases of your retirement years, so it's best to prepare accordingly. Some people avoid long-term care planning because they think they can handle the costs. They believe they'll be in a lower tax bracket, won't be working, and will have more money to spend. This can be a devastating mistake.

For those who do prepare, there are several traditional methods of long-term care planning available. Major flaws exist, however, so let's take a detailed look at them in this section.

Medicare and Medicaid

If you're thinking I had the Williams apply for Medicare or Medicaid, that wasn't the case. While people can apply for Medicaid and Medicare, that in and of itself is not an adequate long-term care plan.

Most people know or understand Medicare and Medicaid to some degree. They often have a vague idea that these government programs will take care of them if something happens. But those programs don't pay for everything.

Everyone has to sign up for Medicare when they turn sixty-five in the United States. If you get sick before age sixty-five or become disabled, then you can apply for Medicare early. Medicaid, on the other hand, is a whole different program. It's a means-tested program, meaning you have to use your own resources first before you can qualify. At that point, Medicaid covers part of your expenses if you have to go to a nursing home.

Medicaid and Medicare work together to pay nursing home expenses for people who don't have any savings. Medicaid pays for the actual room someone lives in—the rent of the nursing home itself. Medicare pays for the doctor visits, prescription drugs, and other types of care.

If you have a nest egg of some sort, and you want to apply for Medicaid to help you in a long-term care facility, you might be out of luck. Your reserves can be drained, and in some cases, they can empty quickly. Medicaid and Medicare can be part of a long-term care solution, but they're not all-encompassing.

Long-Term Care Policies

If Medicaid and Medicare won't cut it, what about long-term care policies? These policies are designed to cover your expenses if you need long-term care, as the name implies. On the surface, they seem to fit the bill, but I don't usually recommend them, for several reasons.

One problem with long-term care policies is that you have to qualify, and long-term care policies are underwritten for your health. It's almost like an auto insurance policy where you have to pay a premium every month or every year, and you get charged extra for every mark on your driving record. So unless you're in excellent health, you may not qualify for such a policy.

Another problem with long-term care policies is that they can be prohibitively expensive for one person. They can cost anywhere from $2,000 to $5,000 a year. The more bells and whistles you add, like inflation protection and other features, the more expensive they become. And like auto insurance, that money is out the door once you've paid it, even if you never use the policy. If you never get in a car accident or never use the long-term care policy, then you're out those funds for good. That's the nature of insurance policies.

Life Insurance Riders

Let's circle back to the Williams. After Mr. Williams had his stroke, Mrs. Williams and I had to go back to the drawing board. We revamped their retirement plan to start generating some income two years earlier than planned so they could pay for some of the in-home care Mr. Williams needed. It wasn't going to be enough, or it wasn't what we had planned, but we began to fix things by starting Mr. Williams's income on his retirement plan.

Since Mr. Williams was no longer working and was forced into retirement, he took his pension from his company. This provided the couple with some income. Looking at their finances, the pair also decided to downsize their home and move into something a lot smaller. They used the proceeds from the sale of their home for future care.

Finally, the type of annuity we selected for this new plan included a feature called a *well-being rider*. This rider kicks in if something happens and you become unable to perform two activities of daily living, which the industry calls ADLs. If this occurs, you qualify under this annuity provision to double your income for five years. The doubled income from the annuity can help pay for those in-home care costs. It's not a long-term fix for a client, but it is a short-term solution. Well-being riders can make a huge difference, especially if something happens without warning.

Mr. Williams passed away about four years after his stroke. At that point, Mrs. Williams came to see me again. It was time for more changes to her financial plan. We looked at the proceeds from the sale of the house plus the remaining proceeds from Mr. Williams's annuity, and we ended up deciding on a two-pronged plan. First, we generated another fixed index annuity in Mrs. Williams's name with a lifetime guaranteed payout. Then, with the excess money, we bought her a life insurance policy with a special rider: a long-term care rider.

Long-Term Care Riders

Today, life insurance policies often have long-term care riders. If you do have to enter a long-term care facility, and you have a long-term care rider, you can use it to pay for your care. Essentially, you convert the death benefit of the life insurance policy into cash to help cover long-term care costs. It's a relatively inexpensive way to generate money, and it's tax-free because it comes from a life insurance policy intended to assist with long-term care expenses.

By combining an annuity that provides guaranteed lifetime income with a life insurance policy that can generate income from the death benefit, you get an effective solution to the long-term care problem. If you never need to go to a nursing home, the death benefit will go tax-free to your beneficiaries. That is what we set up for Mrs. Williams.

This is not a well-known method, but it is preferred in the industry over purchasing a long-term care policy. It can be a better deal because you or your heirs receive the benefit regardless, unlike with a long-term care policy. Once I explain this to clients, more people than not opt to consider some form of permanent life insurance plan for long-term care. This was the case for Mrs. Williams. Since she was a few years younger and in good health, she easily qualified for life insurance. The key here is to get life insurance when you're younger and theoretically in good health.

Pulaskies and Retirement Plans

That day in the Alaskan bush, I didn't think I would cut my leg. That day at work, Mr. Williams didn't think he would have a stroke. But these things happen, and when they do, you have to be prepared. If you have a health crisis and haven't planned ahead, your retirement accounts can empty fast. Traditionally, people rely on government programs and long-term care policies to cover these expenses, but Medicare and Medicaid often don't cover enough of this care, and long-term care policies are pricey and not always an option, depending on your health.

That's why I'm such a fan of riders on permanent life insurance policies. In Mr. Williams's situation, we used a well-being rider that doubled his income for five years. For more comprehensive planning, you can use a long-term care rider on a life insurance policy to help you pay for care without buying a policy that you may never use. If you never go to the long-term care facility, then obviously the life insurance policy's full death benefit goes to the beneficiaries. If you do go to a long-term care facility, you have the provision to help pay for that. It's a win-win, and it's my recommended method for ensuring you're not stranded if the worst should happen. When the Williams did initial planning, they refused the life insurance option because they were healthy and didn't see the point. In the end, it worked out for Mrs. Williams because, fortunately, she was still in good health. After what she went through, she could see the benefit of life insurance and long-term care.

CHAPTER 7

WHEN LIGHTNING STRIKES—ESTATE AND LEGACY PLANNING

Massive fire front burning in the tree crown.

Cottonwood trees, aspen trees, and birch trees—anything in the poplar family—absorb a lot of moisture. Firefighters can retreat or withdraw to poplars, which provide some sanctuary from a fire. This little fact saved my life in the San Juan National Forest near Durango, Colorado, at an elevation of approximately nine thousand feet. But even a safe haven can't protect you from the wrath of God.

I was in the San Juan National Forest, based out of Dolores, Colorado. My crew and I were working a fire near La Plata Peak, a 14,000-foot peak outside Durango. This fire was approximately a hundred acres, large enough to have several crews assigned to different sections.

We were digging a handline to circle the fire, battling the roots in the dense forest, when it started to cloud over. A thunderstorm was coming, which often happens in the summer, and we all knew what that meant. When a thunderstorm swirls the wind currents around, you get high, unpredictable winds that can come from any direction. It makes for a dangerous environment when you can't predict which way the wind might blow the fire.

"Crew, pull back!" the crew boss shouted. "Head for that grove of aspen trees."

Patches of aspen sporadically grow throughout those woods, creating a mosaic between the spruce and fir trees. When it's not on fire, it's stunning. We all retreated into the nearby grove of aspen. I looked around at these monstrous trees, probably fifteen to twenty inches in diameter and anywhere from sixty to eighty feet tall.

We should be okay here, I thought. Then the deluge began. It was raining cats and dogs. Despite the heavy downpour, we were somewhat sheltered beneath our raincoats. We hunkered down, feeling as good as possible under the circumstances, when lightning struck.

No more than maybe thirty or forty yards away, the lightning directed right into a tall aspen. I saw the light and the flash—and the tree exploded. Shattered to smithereens, like it had been hit with a bomb. The ground shook. I mean, that *boom*—you can feel it in your chest. It's unforgettable, and I hope you never feel it.

The firefighters buzzed into action, confirming everyone's safety. The proximity of the strike meant that injuries were a real possibility, and with everything soaked from the rain, there was significant risk of electricity traveling through the wet ground. Anyone within a considerable radius of that tree could have been hurt.

We got lucky. Everyone was safe, and the rain eventually abated and stopped. We had survived the storm.

I never forgot that experience because we really thought we were okay. We had retreated into what was supposed to be a haven from the fire and the storm. We were proven wrong in the most violent way. Lightning can hit any tree you're sitting under, even an aspen. It was a random event, and it was nearly fatal.

Now, let's talk about your retirement. You might carefully plan every little thing, setting up an annuity ladder, diversifying, and shoring up your safe haven until it's as secure as can be. But sometimes life can be unpredictable, and you never know when your retirement will come to an end. So even if your retirement plan could sustain you and your spouse until you're both 200 years old, it's smart to take a look at estate planning. This chapter explains how estate planning can benefit both you and your heirs, delineates the probate process, and delves into how financial advisors collaborate with attorneys to craft an estate plan that's perfect for your financial plan.

Understanding the Importance of Legacy Planning

A few years back, two sisters named Jill and Joan hired me as their retirement planner. These unmarried sisters were inseparable and lived across the street from each other in a small community. They each had their own retirement funds and money, and they each wanted to name the other as their sole heir and beneficiary.

I helped both sisters by arranging an annuity and planning some retirement details. As part of this, I performed a fact-finder process to gather all the information I could about each sister's financial situation. This is an important part of my client onboarding process in general. I asked each sister for the details of their assets, including bank accounts, real estate, trusts, and anything else they might be holding on to. This ensures that any recommendations I make are based on complete financial information. It's also crucial for estate planning specifically because when you don't have a beneficiary listed on a financial account, serious problems can arise later.

I carefully questioned each sister about their assets, then created a plan for each. I didn't see them for a year, at which point Joan gave me a call.

"Jill passed," Joan said tearfully. "Can I make an appointment to see you?"

When Joan came in several weeks later, she brought a folder full of Jill's financial papers. When we looked into these materials, we discovered a surprise: Jill had oil rights to a rig in Oklahoma from a deceased spouse. She hadn't told me about that, and this account didn't have any listed beneficiary.

"From a legal standpoint, when there's no beneficiary," I said to Joan, "you don't have any way of knowing what someone wanted to do with their money. A probate judge will have to decide where those funds go."

"But Jill and I had an agreement," Joan said. "You know that. She meant for me to inherit all her assets. We talked about it a million times."

"I know," I said sadly. "But legally, that doesn't matter now. It won't matter to the judge."

If you don't plan what happens with your assets, including your home, bank accounts, IRAs, and annuities, it can create issues in the courts or through the probate process. The law states that when there's no named beneficiary for an asset, the courts follow the bloodline. First, they look for a spouse, then they look for immediate descendants, such as children. If there are no children, it looks upward to parents, and if the parents are no longer there, it looks sideways to siblings.

In this particular case, Jill didn't have a spouse, but she did have a daughter with whom she was estranged. I didn't know this daughter existed until after Jill's passing. *Per stirpes* dictates that the daughter is first in line, and the sister is second. The daughter, as expected, fought for the money, and as she had the legal upper hand, she won. If Jill had remembered to disclose this account, things would have turned out very differently for Joan.

As you can see, a lack of planning can quickly turn into a real catfight. This situation involved two people, but sometimes the catfight can involve siblings, parents, and other relatives into the double digits. Most of the time, people forget to name beneficiaries, like Jill did.

But that's only one scenario that can happen if you don't create a proper legacy plan.

Consider another important factor: divorce. During or after a divorce, an estate plan can quickly go sideways. Old beneficiaries—ones who may not even be in the picture anymore—may end up inheriting. Additionally, blended families can create complications. When two people marry and each has children from a prior marriage, it can become contentious if there isn't a plan for managing the estate. This isn't an area of your financial plan you want to ignore if you want a say in who inherits your assets. The key here is to always name the beneficiaries on your assets.

Probate and Legacy Planning

Most of you reading this book are probably old enough to have served as the executor of a will or to know somebody who has. Even if you have some experience with probate, you might not know all the ins and outs of the process. If that's the case, this section will explain how probate works and how it affects legacy planning. Feel free to skip this section if probate is familiar to you.

The process of probate isn't what many people perceive it to be; it's not a tax or a cost. Instead, the probate process is an old system that ensures estates are distributed as fairly as possible. The beginning of the probate process involves a declaration, such as placing a public notice in the obituary section of the local paper. This public notice must be published for around six months, and it invites anyone with an interest in the deceased person's assets or anyone with claims against the estate to come forward. It's essentially a call to arms for anyone with a vested interest, telling them to show up on the date that the probate is executed in court.

During the probate hearing, the judge will open the will, assuming there is one, to see who inherits the assets. The judge then provides room for objections from other interested parties. For example, if two daughters inherit a house, the judge allows anyone in the court to raise objections. If no objections exist, the judge instructs the county clerk to transfer the deed to the daughters. If someone does raise a contention, such as claiming they are owed something, the judge must determine the distribution of assets.

A lot of legacy planning is about making sure your money goes where it's supposed to and also making things as easy as possible for your heirs. Often, this is accomplished by avoiding probate altogether. While avoiding probate is good at times, at other times, it's not the best option.

For example, a will necessitates your assets going through probate, while a trust bypasses the probate process. A trust requires the services of an attorney, and an attorney may charge a considerable amount depending on the complexity of the estate plan. Some individuals may opt not to incur these expenses. Other options exist, but for many, a will is the easiest and most cost-effective route. Regardless of whatever estate planning steps you take, including using annuities as I describe later in this chapter, everyone should have a will.

My Role in Legacy Planning as a Financial Advisor

Some legacy planning matters must be handled by an attorney rather than a financial advisor. Some of what we do overlaps, but when I need to call in an attorney, I do so. Keep in mind that my collaboration with an attorney operates within legal boundaries. Neither the attorney nor I can compensate each other monetarily; there are no finder's fees. We work independently, ensuring there is no illicit exchange of funds.

I have to work independently of the attorney, but we can collaborate to ensure that whatever plan is developed includes everything, including annuities. This allows the client to walk away with a document or a legacy plan that they have designed, dictating exactly how they want their assets distributed.

As a financial advisor, my role in legacy planning starts with the aforementioned fact finding. Asking clients about their assets to get a complete picture of their holdings is an important part of what I do. People are sometimes reluctant to disclose everything, even though they have come to me as a financial advisor. I have to explain that if I don't have all the information, my recommendations may be flawed because they won't include all their assets. The fact-finding process lets me understand the entire picture so that my recommendations are accurate and based on the whole, not the part. Ninety-nine percent of the time, it works, although the occasional Jill does sneak through.

I also work with my clients to integrate legacy planning into their broader financial plans. For example, I often visit couples who have various assets. They might have a range of holdings, including money, IRAs, other accounts, real estate, and rental properties.

"You have a lot of assets here," I might tell them. "What do you want to do with them when you die?"

"We have a will," one of them will say. "We're happy with that."

In that case, I would normally recommend putting that IRA into an annuity. That would generate guaranteed income for as long as the couple needed it.

Now, if one of them tells me, "We have all this stuff, and we don't want to go through probate," or "We want this bit to go to our daughter and this bit to go to our son," then I might say, "Oh, this is complicated. Let me introduce you to the attorney I work with." The attorney and I would then meet with them, and the attorney would generate an estate plan.

In that scenario, the attorney and I may determine that if we put the IRA money into an annuity to generate income for life, we could include that in the plan the attorney might devise. This could be either through a will or a trust, depending on the client's preferences. The attorney works independently to create this legal document that states what will happen to their assets, and I take care of the rest of the financial planning.

Annuities and Legacy Planning

If you do a good job creating a legacy plan, you can ensure that your beneficiaries inherit what you want them to inherit without extra hassle, fighting, or fees. Often, annuities can be incorporated as part of a retirement plan that becomes a strong legacy plan. For example, I have a client named Emily whose father passed away.

"My mom's in her nineties," Emily told me at the time. "She's in assisted living and needs some income. What can we do to help her? And how can we ensure that any leftover money passes on to me and my brother down the road?"

Emily brought in a comprehensive list of her mother's assets, and we set up an annuity. The money was generating interest, and since the mom didn't need the funds at the time, she wasn't withdrawing any money from it. Instead, it was accumulating in growth or interest, ready to be used when it was needed.

Shortly after we got the annuity set up, lo and behold, Emily's mother fell ill and passed away unexpectedly. Despite her age, Emily's mother had been in good health, so this came as a shock. When Emily came to see me again, I was glad not to add to her burden. Unlike other assets, annuities are a product that, by law, completely bypass probate. They are not part of the probate process. I helped Emily fill out the forms to have that money immediately directed to her. Since the funds were not IRA funds but regular savings, Emily was allowed by law to take that money and use it elsewhere.

This is certainly not the only scenario in which good estate planning can help, but it's an excellent example. There was no contention, no one claiming they should have been a beneficiary, no drawn-out probate possible. Emily's case also involves something called *cost basis upon death*, which I would like to take a moment to explain.

Cost Basis upon Death

A cost basis upon death is a legal stipulation that applies to most assets, such as houses and cars. The IRS states that on the date of death, the value of any asset owned by the deceased has to be assessed. That amount is not taxable if the asset is sold later, but any increase in value is considered capital gains and is taxed as such.

For instance, let's say you inherit a piece of property. The moment the person who left you the property dies, the legal cost basis is established. You don't sell the property immediately and instead wait until several years later. By then, the property is worth more. Any increase in value from the date of death to the date of sale is considered capital gains, and the IRS expects you to pay taxes on it.

Annuity money is not capital gains taxed, but it works similarly in that you have to pay taxes only on earnings. Annuity funds, however, are taxed based on the gain since the funds were put in rather than a death date. For example, if someone puts in $100,000, and it grows to $120,000 before you inherit, you have to pay taxes on the $20,000 rather than the whole amount. Legally, this amount is considered income rather than a capital gain and can therefore be taxed at a different rate.

If you have to pay taxes on gains either way, what's the difference between inheriting property and annuities? It's simple: Annuity money is available to you as soon as you inherit it. You can withdraw a little or a lot, as much as you want, as quickly as you want. Meanwhile, the rest of the annuity will continue to grow. On the other hand, you have to go through the whole process of selling the property to get any liquid funds, and as soon as you do that, the property is gone. It's a much more laborious process, and you then need to figure out what to do with whatever funds you have left over. The annuity creates no work and provides more flexibility to heirs.

In Emily's case, since it was an annuity, she was able to collect the money without going through probate. There was a small amount of interest earned on the annuity, and she received the money seamlessly without added taxes.

Leaving a Lightning-Proof Legacy

It is generally known in the firefighting world that the aspen tree contains too much water to burn well. Aspens love water, and its wood has one of the highest water contents of any species in the forest. Similarly, you now know that an annuity is a safe way to guarantee income for life. It can keep you provided for and thriving for years and years. But even that doesn't stop lightning when it strikes, and nothing can change the fact that, eventually, we all move on from this life.

A lack of legacy planning can leave a real mess for loved ones, creating tension between family members. It can be a major problem if you don't plan your legacy. On the other hand, including a legacy plan in your retirement planning helps you feel secure. You'll know that your estate will go to the people and causes you care about rather than being randomly distributed through probate. Whether you opt for a simple will or a more detailed plan requiring an attorney, legacy planning is the final step of financial preparedness that you need for a truly fireproof retirement plan.

Fire burning intensely into the night.

CONCLUSION

When you think of a fire, you usually think of a big conflagration that's hard to miss. But in my career, I encountered a lot of fires that were hidden in huge forests and needed to be literally sniffed out. I did this countless times to the point that I became good at bushwhacking only using a map, a compass, and my sense of smell. We called this process of finding the fire the "Initial Attack." Toward the end of my career, GPS changed all that.

There's an eerie feeling you get when you're hiking in a pitch-black environment, looking for a fire. You're walking blind through a tangled forest, trying to catch a whiff of smoke to guide you to the fire you need to put out. It takes skill to get over that feeling and master the technique.

Most people would know better than to try to find a forest fire in the dark like that on their own. It's not safe, and the risks are too many. When it comes to retirement planning, though, many people think they can handle it themselves. The truth is that there is far too much at stake here for you to treat it as a DIY project. This is your livelihood we're talking about—your ability to support yourself and your spouse for life, even in the face of fire. That's not something you want to blindly stumble into.

That's why I urge you to seek assistance from a professional. We can ask the questions that you may not even know to ask, helping you avoid any hidden hazards. I'm a Certified Financial Fiduciary and hold an Ed Slott Master Elite IRA certification. I've been sniffing out these financial fires for years, and I'm well-qualified and would love to help you. But if you don't contact me, at least reach out to a retirement planner or estate planner who specializes in this field. Only a financial firefighter can help you create your fireproof retirement plan.

Remember: Smokey says, "Only you can prevent wildfires." I say, "Only you can prevent retirement fires."

After the fire storm there is lingering evidence of its intensity.

BIBLIOGRAPHY

"1988 Fires." Yellowstone National Park (US National Park Service)." Accessed March 27, 2024. https://www.nps.gov/yell/learn/nature/1988-fires.htm.

"Annual Estimates of the Resident Population for Selected Age Groups by Sex for the United States: April 1, 2020 to July 1, 2022." US Census Bureau. Accessed March 28, 2024. https://www2.census.gov/programs-surveys/popest/tables/2020-2022/national/asrh/nc-est2022-agesex.xlsx.

Arias, Elizabeth. "United States Life Tables, 2004." National Vital Statistics Reports. December 28, 2007. https://www.cdc.gov/nchs/data/nvsr/nvsr56/nvsr56_09.pdf.

Blanchett, David; Michael Finke, and Wade D. Pfau. "Low Bond Yields and Safe Portfolio Withdrawal Rates." Morningstar Investment Management. January 21, 2013. https://s3.amazonaws.com/static.contentres.com/media/documents/6bc2b7ed-8f1c-4f33-8f81-d8db3fb444fe.pdf.

Contributor, Impact Partners. "How Does Sequence of Returns Risk Impact Your Retirement?" *Forbes.* July 22, 2019. https://www.forbes.com/sites/impactpartners/2019/07/22/how-does-sequence-of-returns-risk-impact-your-retirement/?sh=7d23d54b50ee.

"Current US Inflation Rates: 2000–2024," US Inflation Calculator, accessed March 12, 2024, https://www.usinflationcalculator. com/inflation/current-inflation-rates.

"IRS Provides Tax Inflation Adjustments for Tax Year 2024." Internal Revenue Service. Accessed April 12, 2024. https://www.irs.gov/newsroom/ irs-provides-tax-inflation-adjustments-for-tax-year-2024.

Konish, Lorie. "As Baby Boomers Hit 'Peak 65' This Year, What the Retirement Age Should Be Is Up for Debate." CNBC. February 8, 2024. https://www.cnbc.com/2024/02/08/ baby-boomers-hit-peak-65-in-2024-why-retirement-age-is-in-question.html.

"Life Expectancy and Healthy Life Expectancy at Age 65." Health at a Glance 2017: OECD Indicators. OECD Publishing. https://doi.org/10.1787/health_glance-2017-74-en.

"Life Expectancy at 65." OECD. Accessed March 29, 2024. https://data.oecd.org/healthstat/life-expectancy-at-65.htm.

"LIMRA: US Annuity Sales Post Another Record Year in 2023." Accessed May 5, 2024. https://www. limra.com/en/newsroom/news-releases/2024/ limra-u.s.-annuity-sales-post-another-record-year-in-2023/.

Peters, Daniel A., and D. A. McKay. "Life insurance: Ownership and Investment Considerations." *Plastic Surgery (Oakville, Ont.).* 22(1). (2014): 54–55. https://www.ncbi.nlm.nih.gov/ pmc/articles/PMC4128435/.

"Retirement & Survivors Benefits: Life Expectancy Calculator." Social Security Administration. Accessed March 3, 2024. https://www.ssa.gov/cgi-bin/longevity.cgi.

"Tom Hegna." Facebook. January 28, 2020. https://web.facebook. com/TomHegnaSpeaks/posts/2779911268783210/.

Wollman Rusoff, Jane. "Wade Pfau: Pandemic Tears Up 4% Rule." *ThinkAdvisor.* February 10, 2021. https://www.thinkadvisor.com/2020/04/14/ wade-pfau-virus-crisis-has-slashed-4-rule-nearly-in-half/.

ABOUT THE AUTHOR

For more than two decades, **AL MARTINEZ** has been an advisor and general agent in the financial services industry, helping clients make sound financial decisions in insurance and retirement planning.

As the host of the *Retirement & Income* Radio Show, his focus is on providing safe money retirement strategies and solutions, exploring ways to protect retirement money, increase income, and protect against potential market losses and economic volatility, including health circumstances, taxes, and those unforeseen situations that can be devastating to principal assets in retirement.

During his previous career as a fire specialty officer, Al protected firefighters by developing and implementing fire safety training. Now he extends the same idea of protection to finances. Al helps people retire with safety and security, by finding financial solutions to protect their hard-earned and precious retirement assets.

Recently Al has expanded his services to include a program called Debt Free 4 Life, which is designed to help people get out of debt.

www.ingramcontent.com/pod-product-compliance
Lightning Source LLC
Chambersburg PA
CBHW071425210326
41597CB00020B/3654